A COORDINATOR'S GUIDE TO HELP AMERICA READ

A Handbook for Volunteers

Gay Su Pinnell and Irene C. Fountas

HEINEMANN
Portsmouth, NH

Heinemann
A division of Reed Elsevier Inc.
361 Hanover Street
Portsmouth, NH 03801-3912

Offices and agents throughout the world

Library of Congress Cataloging-in-Publication Data
CIP is on file with the Library of Congress.
ISBN 0-435-07252-8

Editor: Lois Bridges
Production: Renée Le Verrier and Melissa L. Inglis
Cover design: Barbara Werden
Manufacturing: Louise Richardson

Printed in the United States of America on acid-free paper
01 00 99 98 97   ML   1 2 3 4 5 6 7 8 9

Contents

Acknowledgments

I f we are to achieve literacy for all, many individuals must contribute their time and expertise. We salute those who give their time and attention to supporting young children in the critical beginnings of literacy—volunteers who work with children as well as those who organize and lead their efforts.

We also recognize and express our appreciation to enlightened community leaders who see the need for this work. In particular, the Charles A. Dana Foundation, the Martha Holden Jennings Foundation, and the Noyce Foundation have, over the years, consistently supported teachers and children in literacy efforts such as Reading Recovery, the Early Literacy Learning Initiative, and AmeriCorps for Math and Literacy. These leadership efforts, supported and guided by service oriented foundations, have provided a resource for the work in *Help America Read: A Handbook for Volunteers* and *A Coordinator's Guide to Help America Read*.

We wish to acknowledge the inspiration of Uri Treisman, who involved us in service, and of Mike Gibbons, who saw the need for this book. We also appreciate the vision of Penny Noyce, Ann Bowers, and Joan Wylie of the Noyce Foundation in their work for comprehensive literacy education.

We acknowledge our colleagues Diane DeFord, Sue Constable, Colleen Griffiths, and Janet George, whose exemplary work with AmeriCorps members has provided a model for service every day. Additionally, we thank all of the outstanding educators involved in the Early Literacy Learning Initiative, on which we have based our suggestions for volunteers and coordinators. Andrea McCarrier, Justina Henry, Mary Fried, Joan Wiley, Sue Hundley, Diane Powell,

Carol Lyons, Diane DeFord, and others have provided the leadership for this important effort and we thank them. We also express appreciation to our colleagues in Reading Recovery, in particular Billie Askew, Carol Lyons, and Diane DeFord, educators who always have foremost in mind the literacy achievement of children who, through no fault of their own, may be at risk in school settings. Our colleagues' work, on behalf of literacy for all children, is an example of the commitment we need in order to fulfill the goals of America Reads.

Our office staff have worked especially hard to make both volumes possible and we heartily acknowledge their contributions here. Polly Taylor provided organizational support in many ways; Heather Kroll, Erika Hession, Jennifer Warner, and Karen Travelo also gave generously of their support.

To our families, we express special thanks, especially to Ron Melhado, Bill Wayson, and Elfrieda Pinnell who encouraged us throughout the process. We also thank the children who provided writing samples for our use.

Preparing two volumes simultaneously is a daunting task and it could not have been accomplished without the expertise and diligence of the Heinemann staff. Without the work of our editor, Lois Bridges, this book would not have been possible. We have sincerely valued her partnership in this entire venture. Renée Le Verrier's expertise and creativity, Melissa Inglis' attention to detail and finishing touches, and Mike Gibbons' positive encouragement were all essential.

And for the work this volume represents, we thank the volunteer leaders who will make it possible for all of us to give our best to children.

Introduction

Volunteers symbolize our nation's commitment to children. As a volunteer leader, you put that commitment to work.

This guide is designed to help those who coordinate and lead other volunteers as they build and implement a high-quality service program in any setting. You may be a volunteer yourself, who is able to commit your time and expertise to organize and support a group of other volunteers. You may be a school staff member, a community agency director, a youth group leader, or a church member who wants to ensure that the volunteers in your program work effectively with students. This guide offers suggestions for coordinating all aspects of the program and also for using the handbook, *Help America Read: A Handbook for Volunteers*, as the core resource for meaningful, effective training.

Help America Read: A Handbook for Volunteers is intended to support literacy volunteers in their work with young children. Parents, teachers, community members, and volunteers share the goal of helping every child become a competent, independent reader and writer by the third grade. The handbook provides practical information about getting started, and describes in detail ten effective ways of supporting literacy learning with children from preschool through grade three. Each chapter is clear and easy to understand. Volunteers will find specific sets of guidelines and directions for working with children as well as specific tools they can use right away such as lists of good books, lists of words for letter and word study, handwriting charts, and spelling tools. We provide examples, photographs, and drawings to illustrate concepts. We also ask volunteers to evaluate their own work through questions at the end of each chapter.

Today, there are tens of thousands of children who need extra attention from adults. Our future, tied as it is to advanced technology, demands high levels of reading and writing skills for almost all workers. Rudimentary or minimal skills are not enough. Reaching advanced levels means that children must get the "basics" at an early age and learn to read and write on their own.

Literacy volunteers can give children special attention that invites them into the world of books and written language and helps them realize what an important part reading and writing will play in their lives. Literacy volunteers not only demonstrate reading and writing, they demonstrate citizenship. Through their example, students learn what it means to give to others.

Volunteering should be valuable and enjoyable for everyone— students and volunteers alike. Our experience has shown us, again and again, that volunteers discover many rewards in their work with children. The time volunteers dedicate to service is precious. You, as the coordinator, will want to help them work efficiently with children and make the most of every moment. In *Help America Read* and in this guide, we describe effective volunteer activities that you can organize with minimal effort.

Volunteers cannot take the place of teachers, nor should they assume responsibility for teaching children to read and write. But focused, well-planned volunteer service can greatly enhance a child's learning. Your contribution as the leader and coordinator of these efforts is invaluable to the school or community center in which you and others volunteer. It is our pleasure and privilege to offer this guidebook to assist you in your leadership work.

What Makes an Effective Volunteer Program?

Thirty years ago, most volunteers were the mothers of young children. Today, things have changed. As a literacy volunteer coordinator, it's likely that you will work with a wide range of volunteers from college students to business executives. Some volunteers will devote as much as fifteen to twenty hours a week to their volunteer work. Others will have limited time. The volunteer program must be flexible enough to accommodate different scheduling arrangements but structured enough to be effective and make a difference for children. As the coordinator, your primary goal is to create a program that works well for students and volunteers alike. In this chapter, we present the key principles, drawn from research and our own experiences, that govern effective volunteer programs.

What Does the Research Say?

In 1990, the Committee on the Use of Volunteers in Schools (Bernard 1991) surveyed the research on school volunteer programs and their impact. Bernard found that tutored students made academic gains greater than might have been expected and greater than those students who were not tutored. Additionally, tutored students grew in their confidence and self-esteem. Drawing from his review of volunteer programs, Bernard also defined the characteristics of successful volunteer programs. He found that all successful programs featured:

■ Sound organization and management.
■ Support from "the top" or administrative level.
■ Close cooperation between volunteers and people in the school.
■ Clear expectations; the volunteers knew exactly what was expected of them.

Wasik (1997) recently examined dozens of volunteer programs designed to help young children in literacy. She studied the characteristics of each program and their results. Synthesizing her research, Wasik outlined eight characteristics of good literacy volunteer programs. DeFord (1996) and Lyons (1995) also studied a volunteer program that provided extensive training and data on children's achievement. DeFord identified characteristics that make a program work and Lyons studied the effect on the volunteers themselves.

Implementing Volunteer Programs

Our conclusion from reading the research is that volunteer programs make an important contribution to children's literacy learning if they are carefully organized and provide high-quality training. The key person is the volunteer leader or coordinator who knows how to make the most of the extra help volunteers offer. The following actions are critical for implementing effective volunteer programs.

Acquire expert help.

As you plan the program, and train and supervise volunteers, ask the pros for help and advice. Wasik (1997) specifically recommends that a reading specialist coordinate and supervise the volunteer program in literacy. If possible, put this person in charge of the program. If you are not a trained reading specialist or if you have not worked with children in many of the ways we outline here, what should you do?

■ Spend time reading *Help America Read*.

■ Draw on your related experiences with children; for example, your parenting or camp counseling experiences.

■ Build your expertise before you initiate the volunteer program and continue to work with children while you develop the program.

■ Ask colleagues to observe you and help you evaluate your work with children. You can also involve people with particular expertise in teaching reading and writing; these experts can contribute to the training that you provide volunteers both at the beginning and later, as your volunteers gain experience and ask new questions.

Provide ongoing training.

Provide structured, high-quality training to volunteers not just at the beginning of the program, but, ideally, throughout the program as well. Wasik found that volunteers were most expert when they received good training in the beginning, with subsequent training as they gained experience. The essential element of good training will make the tutoring difference.

Demonstrate, observe, and coach.

As volunteers observe you, demonstrate how to work effectively with children. Also, "coach" individual volunteers while they work with children. The best training sessions are tailored to the needs and strengths of the volunteers. Training sessions increase the skill of volunteers over time. The end result is tutoring sessions that are more productive for the children and satisfying for the volunteer. When you observe a volunteer, be specific as you talk about particular children, the books they read, what they write, and how to help them. Volunteers find on-the-job feedback extremely helpful.

Encourage volunteers to reflect on their work.

Invite volunteers think about their work in a way that helps them deepen their understandings of how children learn to read and write. We want volunteers to acquire practical knowledge that will encourage them to make decisions based on understanding rather than following scripts or sets of directions. In this way they'll learn to match their tutoring to the needs of each child.

As volunteers work with child after child, they will learn more about literacy development and how children develop reading and writing abilities. They will also learn as they share their experiences with other volunteers. You can devote part of your training sessions to sharing among volunteers. *Help America Read* provides sets of questions that will help you make group sharing successful.

Provide basic frameworks that volunteers can use in their work with children. Chapter 12 of *Help America Read* includes sample plans that develop the ten ways of working with children (a list of the ten ways is shown in Fig. 2–1 of this guide). Help volunteers plan structured, organized tutoring sessions. Just showing up to tutor is not nearly as effective as tutoring that has been thoughtfully planned beforehand.

Strive for consistent service.

If you want to make a difference for individual children, try to designate enough time for each child to work with the same volunteer. Wasik (1997) recommends a minimum of one and one-half to two hours per week; she also says that children learn best when they are tutored by the same person each time. So plan your schedule for volunteers accordingly. Keep in mind that volunteers also find their work more rewarding when they come to know particular children and can watch them develop over time.

Include many opportunities for reading and writing.

Tutoring sessions that include a lot of reading and writing are most effective when students can use reading and writing for real reasons. Our sample plans show how to put together an intensive thirty-minute or forty-five-minute session with an individual child, combining reading and writing in several different ways. Children also spend a few minutes on phonics, letters, and sounds, as well as activities that help them discover how words work. We do *not* advocate meaningless drills. We use a wide range of quality books and meaningful writing experiences because we believe that children learn to read by reading and to write by writing.

Gather quality materials.

You'll want to provide high-quality materials as well. In an organized program, volunteers will have access to clearly identified quality materials. You will want to have many good books that volunteers can read and reread with children. You will also need writing supplies. Before inviting volunteers to participate, carefully consider the materials you need and begin to collect them. Where budgets are tight, supplies and materials will be at a premium. Learn to be resourceful in securing donations from community supporters. We offer suggestions in *Help America Read* for gathering free materials and organizing them so that they are used well.

Make sure volunteers are dependable and successful.

As coordinator, your role is to ensure that the volunteers are successful. Monitor their attendance and their use of time, space, and materials so that you can offer helpful suggestions early in the program. Help volunteers recognize their success and their contributions. Offering support and praise will enable them to realize their value and encourage them to continue. The more they recognize their contributions, the more time they will want to give. They'll realize their time is making a difference for children.

Monitor the progress of children.

It is the volunteer's job to help children experience success with reading and writing. Whether you are working with children in a school setting or elsewhere, you need to determine whether the volunteer services are actually helping children. It is not necessary to collect extensive data, but do keep lists of books that children can read or lists of words they know how to write. If volunteers create these lists for the children with whom they work, they can discuss their data with you. You can also find ways to communicate with children's teachers. In *Help America Read*, we suggest many ways of sharing information between teachers and volunteers. We also suggest ways to keep progress records.

You'll find these principles helpful as you begin to plan your volunteer program. According to Wasik (1997), "Any tutoring program can provide the tutor and child with a rewarding, positive experience, and can give the child a valued mentor and friend. However, to have tutoring result in real gains in students' reading skills, more structured training, supervision, and planning are needed. With this, volunteer tutoring programs can make a significant difference in the lives of at risk children." In the following chapters in this guide, we expand the principles and also provide guidelines for using *Help America Read*.

Starting a Literacy Volunteer Program

I s recruiting volunteers the first step in starting a volunteer program? No. Good organizers and planners begin by clarifying the nature and characteristics of the volunteer program. Eventually, you'll recruit and train volunteers, making sure that volunteers are well-placed and well-used as a key to effective service.

Before you recruit and train volunteers, consider these basics:

■ Decide who the volunteers will be and with whom they will work.

■ Think about what volunteers will do and the training they may need to do it.

■ Find ways to communicate and work together to make sure the volunteer program is successful.

Identifying and Placing Volunteers

As the coordinator, you will identify and place volunteers where they will be most effective.

Who will benefit from the service of volunteers?

All children can benefit from the service of volunteers. Attention from adults greatly increases children's chances to learn. Volunteers play an important role in creating the educational systems that will support all our children. Consider the following three situations.

First, many of our schools are located in high-poverty areas where children have limited access to books and broad life experiences. Extra adult attention and assistance can make a difference for every child in these settings.

Second, every classroom in the United States has some children who are at risk of failure in reading and writing. Being at risk of failure means that somehow the system has not provided the level of support that these children need to become strong readers and writers. For children at risk of failure in the system, we recommend powerful early intervention programs like Reading Recovery[1] as part of the school's comprehensive

---

[1]Reading Recovery is a tutoring program for first-grade children who are having difficulty learning to read and write. A specially trained teacher provides skilled, daily, thirty-minute lessons for twelve to twenty weeks. Instruction immerses children in extensive reading and writing and teachers help them develop the strategies that good readers and writers use. Research results of the program are excellent, with the great majority of students making accelerated progress. For more information on Reading Recovery, see articles in the reference list for this volume or contact Reading Recovery Council of North America, 1929 Kenny Road, Columbus, OH 43210.

program. Volunteers can make early intervention programs more effective by providing time for talk and practice. Children who have been successful in intervention programs still remain vulnerable in many ways; volunteers can continue to support them.

Third, there are also many schools without the resources for early intervention programs. In these settings, volunteers may be the only source of extra help.

When in a child's life will a literacy partner be most effective?

Our greatest opportunity for successful literacy for all children lies in offering effective support early in children's school careers. The best predictor of school failure is reading below grade level in third grade. To achieve proficiency by third grade, young learners must have thoughtful support in the first three years of their schooling.

What role in a child's learning does the volunteer play?

Volunteers have an important role in the school literacy program. In good schools, you'll find a team approach to success in literacy. The school staff and community view each group of children as their own; they are partners in the success of all. So, becoming a volunteer means entering into a partnership with the teacher and others concerned with children's progress in reading and writing. Volunteers do not take over the role of the teacher or perform the same tasks; they work with teachers so that the child's literacy experiences are expanded.

Who can be a literacy volunteer?

Literacy volunteers can include a wide variety of individuals such as family members (parents, grandparents, caregivers), older students, business people, and retirees. All it takes is a willingness to give time on a regular basis to work with children.

What will volunteers do and what training do they need?

Once you have discussed where you need volunteers and the kind of volunteers who will work best, match them to the needs of children. The central goal of your planning is to make sure that your program produces results in terms of children's learning. You and your colleagues need to think about how best to use the invaluable resources of volunteer time, enthusiasm, and effort.

How can volunteers effectively use their time?

Volunteers have limited time. We have to be sure that their time is well-used and pays off for the children. Volunteers are most helpful when they enhance the work of teachers. They give practice and individual attention that helps children develop ease and enjoyment in reading and writing.

What will volunteers do?

Deciding what volunteers will do means making a complex match between what children need, what volunteers would like to do, and the time, space, and materials available to support the program. Above all, be flexible in making your decisions, and counsel staff members to strive for flexibility as well. As a coordinator, help volunteers become resourceful and independent. The more they work in the setting, the greater knowledge they will have. They will also build credibility with the staff and children. Volunteers will find *Help America Read: A Handbook for Volunteers* a useful resource. Encourage them to read it thoroughly and to use it as a constant reference, rereading sections as they work with children in different ways. As coordinator, you will also want to read the handbook and use it as a reference.

In *Help America Read*, we describe ten ways that volunteers can work effectively with children, and they are represented here in Figure 2–1.

You'll find this chart a helpful organizational tool. As a coordinator of volunteers, it will help if you first talk with people in the service setting about the kinds of things that volunteers can do. Then, it will help you talk with volunteers about what might happen when they work in the school,

Try these ten recommendations for working with children; select them in any order.

Talking with Children
Reading to Children
Reading with Children • Shared Reading
Helping Children Read on Their Own
Writing for Children
Writing with Children • Shared Writing
Helping Children Write on Their Own
Understanding Phonics, Letters, and Words
Making Books
Connecting with Children's Homes

Please refer to Chapter 2 in *Help America Read: A Handbook for Volunteers* for more information on each of these ten ways to help children.

FIGURE 2–1   Ten Ways Literacy Volunteers Can Help Children

library, community center, or other setting. Finally, it will help you plan a good training program and learn to vary the program over time for different purposes.

Work Together Toward a Successful Volunteer Program

Creating a volunteer program is a significant step for a school or other organization to take. It may seem fairly simple to add volunteers to the mix, but, in fact, the presence of any significant number of volunteers changes the setting. Everyone must understand the reasons for the program, the nature of the program, and how the setting will change to accommodate the program.

Who should be involved in planning?
Strive to create a cooperative venture with all involved. In this way, cooperation will build respect and value for the program; everyone will have a stake in its success. If you are coordinating a program in a school or group of schools, you will want to involve all the key players, including:

▌ School principals.
▌ Teachers in whose classrooms volunteers will be working.

▌ Librarians and other people who can provide books and other resources.
▌ Specialists, such as reading teachers, who can contribute to training and supervision.
▌ Members of the parent council.

In other settings, learn which team members can play a role in forming the effort.

How to maintain good communication
Practicing and maintaining effective communication about the volunteer program is similar to every other kind of organizational communication. Before recruiting volunteers, establish a few simple procedures for communication. Here are some examples:

▌ Observe the setting to find the place where people gather to communicate. It might be an office where each staff member has a mailbox. It might be a notice board. Be sure that all communications related to the volunteer program will have a place there.

▌ Establish a simple, one-page newsletter with current information on the program that will go to all staff members and to the volunteers. One volunteer coordinator we know uses her newsletter to recognize volunteers for special efforts, make announcements of events, share training schedules, remind everyone of the school/organizational schedule for events and holidays, and so forth.

❚ Plan orientation sessions for the staff and volunteers. Discuss what to include in the orientation session relative to the specific volunteer setting.

❚ Decide on a system for conveying information to large groups of volunteers (such as a telephone tree).

❚ Identify key staff members who will be your contacts in your role as coordinator.

In conclusion, a team approach to building a volunteer literacy program works best. Thoughtful planning with all key team members and open communication every step of the way will help you create a volunteer program that works for all involved and, most importantly, supports those you and the volunteers are striving to help—the children.

Recruiting and Orienting Volunteers

Once you have organized the program, it is time to recruit and select potential volunteers. We offer some procedural suggestions in this chapter, but keep in mind that your own experience is just as valid. You are ushering volunteers into an existing culture with established relationships and customs. As mentioned in Chapter 2, the volunteers themselves will change that culture as they become part of it. You can help them get a good start as you work with them from the beginning and throughout the duration of the program. In *Help America Read*, you'll find Chapter 1, "Let's Get Started!", especially helpful.

Recruiting Volunteers

As you begin to recruit volunteers, think about personal characteristics that will be most successful in your setting. Volunteers do not need to arrive with extensive training or even experience with young children, although these are certainly desirable. You do want people who:

■ Have energy and commitment.
■ Are flexible.
■ Enjoy children.

■ Are willing to learn new skills and ways of working with children.
■ Like to read and write.
■ Like to work with other people.
■ Enjoy new experiences.
■ Are willing to adjust their schedules to be dependable in their service to children.

You can find individuals who exemplify the above characteristics in many places and in many ways. Where should you look for volunteers? Here are a few suggestions:

■ Retired teachers' associations may have lists of members who want to give service.

■ Senior citizens' living communities may have a group of individuals (including, perhaps, retired teachers) who would enjoy working with children a few hours a week.

■ Colleges and universities may be involved in service learning; preservice teacher-education courses designed to help young people explore teaching are another possible source of volunteers.

■ Local businesses may want to "adopt schools" by sending volunteers.

■ Local service clubs such as Rotary or Lions' Club may involve their members as a service project.

■ Parents and grandparents in the community may be contacted through local schools and invited to participate in a volunteer service program.

■ Churches and synagogues often provide their own tutoring programs, but may also want to contribute to community centers and schools.

■ Public libraries often organize tutoring efforts.

■ High-school students may be involved in service learning programs that bring them into elementary schools during after-school hours or during the summer.

And don't forget the volunteers who are already working with you. They can recruit their friends and family members to provide more service. These volunteers are the best spokespeople for your program.

Children benefit greatly from their contact with an ethnically and racially diverse cross-section of adults in the volunteer setting. Children notice the adults around them and strive to imitate them. If they see people like themselves, they are more likely to emulate their achievements. If possible, recruit a variety of people who reflect different racial and ethnic backgrounds. Multilingual volunteers are especially helpful if your students speak a primary language other than English. Even if children are native English speakers, hearing other languages is invaluable. In addition, you'll want to recruit volunteers of different ages and genders. The group of volunteers can greatly increase a school's capacity to reflect the diversity of our society.

How to recruit qualified volunteers

As you begin recruitment, prepare a simple action plan to guide your activities. Think about actions you want to take and materials you will need, then set up a schedule to accomplish each task you have selected. Here are some suggestions.

1. Create a list of organizations and people you will contact and tell about your program.

2. Prepare a simple, attractive, one-page description of your volunteer program. It's not necessary to include great detail about what volunteers will do, but you can describe the age of children with whom they will work, the probable schedule, and the service volunteers will provide.

3. Request time at organizational meetings (such as local PTA, civic group, retirement community, or church group meetings) to make a short presentation about the need for volunteers and the program you are implementing.

4. Make personal telephone calls to friends and to potential volunteers suggested by others. If the individuals you call can not participate, ask for advice on the program and also for referrals to people who might be interested in participating.

5. Place a notice in newsletters of schools or other organizations. Including a picture of a volunteer and child enjoying their work together helps people visualize what they might accomplish as volunteers.

6. Contact the public relations departments of businesses in your local area. Ask them to assist you in sponsoring and publicizing the program. For example, a slogan like, "one hour to help one child" may capture attention and motivate the business to provide volunteers or donate resources such as books, duplicating services, or paper supplies.

7. Ask a small group of volunteers to assist you with a recruiting plan, if your volunteer program is already underway, and carry out tasks we've outlined here.

8. Ask the person in charge of your local cable television station to post an announcement about your program. Include a telephone number for potential volunteers to call.

9. Contact your local newspaper and ask to place a notice in the community section.

This is not advertising, it's news—so it's free.

10. Invite the local newspaper to write an article about your volunteer program if it's already underway. Ask the reporter to include a phone number for potential volunteers to call.

11. Seek assistance from individuals involved in civic organizations whose membership is composed of varied racial and language groups to help you achieve diversity among the volunteers.

Interviewing and advising literacy volunteers

To assist you with the volunteer selection process, ask potential volunteers to fill out an application. An application informs volunteers of the value of their work. It also gives you valuable information that helps you select and train the volunteers. (See Appendix C: Sample Application.)

The first assistance you can provide potential literacy volunteers is guiding their decision to commit time to the program. Deciding to become a literacy volunteer is serious because once the volunteers begin their work, children look forward to working with their volunteer partners. Just a little work with children will not achieve the desired effect. Both the volunteer and the child need to build their relationship over time, because children learn the skills they need through regular practice. Working with children every day may be impossible for volunteers, but to be most effective they should offer regular, scheduled tutoring.

As much as possible, volunteers should work together to organize their schedules so that their contribution to children is regular and dependable. Consider, also, the tutoring setting. It should be easy for both volunteers and students to reach.

Help potential volunteers reflect on their own personal experiences that they can use to help children learn to read and write. Encourage them to think back to former volunteer work—to relationships with siblings or cousins, to camp counseling or scouting experiences, to church work with children—even to babysitting. Thinking about these experiences will help them decide whether to volunteer, how much time to commit, and what kind of volunteering they will find most successful.

When you interview potential volunteers, here are some questions you can ask to help them make this important decision.

❚ Can I really find the time on a regular basis to work as a literacy volunteer?

❚ Is the location for volunteering convenient to my home or work place so that I do not have to spend too much time traveling?

❚ Do I know from past experiences that I would enjoy working with young children in reading and writing?

❚ Do I like to read or write and do I want to share this enthusiasm with children?

Discuss these questions and others that may arise in an informal interview with the potential volunteer. Since volunteers have little time and most will want to get started right away, we advise you to use the initial interview to settle as much as you can about each volunteer's participation in the program. Some topics you might cover in the interview include:

❚ The nature of volunteering that your program requires.
❚ The time the volunteer will commit and the schedule for service.
❚ Directions to the location that will house the volunteering and training program.
❚ Required commitment for training and the dates and times of training.

As you work with the staff at your place of service, you will learn more specifically what people expect of volunteers. For example,

▌ How should children address volunteers (Mr., Mrs., or first name)?

▌ What are some general guidelines for the way in which volunteers should dress?

▌ Are background checks needed (for example, for volunteers who work in a school)?

▌ Are health certificates needed?

Be sure that the volunteers understand the expectations of their place of service and assist them in meeting the requirements.

Helping Volunteers Get Started

In Chapter 1 of *Help America Read* we provide specific guidelines that will help the volunteer get started in the place of service. These suggestions range from finding out the policies and procedures of the organization, to communicating with the people in charge, to getting to know children and building relationships over time. The handbook also offers specific suggestions to help the volunteer manage time.

Provide an Orientation

Every volunteer will need an orientation to the job and to the setting. Prepare a packet of materials that will serve as a resource. Here are some items to include.

▌ Any material that describes the school, organization, or agency and its mission.
▌ A list of key staff people and important telephone numbers.
▌ A map of the building.
▌ A calendar that shows work days, special occasions, and holidays.
▌ A list of materials available in the building that volunteers can use.
▌ Rules and operating procedures for the building.

We have provided a sample plan for a volunteer orientation session in Appendix A. If you are in a school setting, school representatives should be present for introductions. In addition, you will want to plan a get-together to introduce the volunteers to the entire staff, including teachers. Consider organizing a staff meeting or social. It's a good idea to have an agenda for the orientation, including the items listed in our sample orientation plan (see page 41). If you have time, you may combine the orientation with the first training session. Or, you may schedule training for another time. The first meeting with volunteers should help them feel part of an important group and enable them to get to know each other. After all, the support of colleagues is one important aspect of success. Be sure that the beginning session is organized and engaging, for it will set the tone for the whole program.

Orienting the staff in the place of service

Volunteers are guests in the service setting, so their hosts need orientation as well. Staff members will play various roles in regard to the volunteers, ranging from simply being friendly and knowledgeable hosts to working closely with them and advising them on their work with children. Here are some suggestions for preparing the staff.

▌ Ask staff members if they have any special requests regarding how materials and space are used by volunteers.

▌ Clearly identify a contact person to whom staff members can address questions and express concerns. This might be you as the coordinator or a lead volunteer. Provide telephone numbers when appropriate.

▌ Hold a brief orientation session for all staff members so that you can describe the program and explain what volunteers will be doing. Outline the volunteers' schedules.

▌ For those staff members who will work closely with volunteers, arrange more specific training sessions as needed. For example, the ten ways of helping children with literacy learning described in *Help America Read* may be new and intriguing to librarians, parents, or teachers. You'll want to make sure that they are thoroughly familiar with what volunteers will be doing and why.

∎ Conduct regularly scheduled, brief meetings with staff members who work closely with volunteers so that you can check progress and solve or prevent problems.

∎ Establish a mailbox in the place of service so that staff members can leave you notes about the volunteer program.

∎ Suggest methods of communicating with the volunteers (for example, a notebook or clipboard on which the volunteer and staff member can write notes to each other so they can avoid interruptions while staff members are working with children.)

∎ If you are in a school setting, help the staff understand that a volunteer may not at any time substitute for professional staff. Also, help them realize that volunteers provide extra help for children; they do not substitute for classroom instruction in literacy.

∎ Inform the staff of the training the volunteers will have.

∎ Ask for suggestions from the staff on ways to value volunteers and show them that they are appreciated (for example, recognition breakfasts, special certificates, and general friendliness).

For everyone involved in the volunteer program, ongoing communication is the key to success. The more people work together on behalf of children, the greater the benefit for all involved.

Preparing for the Training Program

Help America Read details ten ways literacy volunteers can work effectively with children. While *Help America Read* offers ongoing support for volunteers, the volunteer organizing agency will want to provide comprehensive training. Indeed, implementing a highly successful program begins with high-quality training for all volunteers.

What are the overarching goals of a strong training program? They are twofold: to help volunteers work successfully with children and to help them make the most of their limited time. With training and good organization, volunteers will

■ Achieve consistent quality.

■ See positive results from their services.

■ Feel personally rewarded from their work with children.

■ Spend their time with children in ways that are efficient and effective.

■ Enjoy respect in their place of service.

■ Learn valuable work and living skills from their participation in the program.

■ Be effective as measured by children's increased achievement in and more positive attitudes toward reading and writing.

The last reason is the primary reason for starting a volunteer program in the first place. It is vital to remember that children need the services of both teachers and volunteers. We have encountered situations, for example, where children were allowed to miss "reading group" with the teacher but not time with a volunteer. Children need both.

A good volunteer program will be organized so that children

■ Do not miss classroom reading and writing instruction.

■ Receive help from well-trained, expert volunteers.

■ Look forward to their time with volunteers.

We also want to emphasize the rewards of service to the volunteers. Service should be a "win-win" situation. If volunteers receive training and participate in a good program, they will develop important skills and understandings that will help them in their future careers and personal lives. Volunteering will enable them to

■ Work more effectively with their own children or grandchildren.

■ Make more thoughtful and knowledgeable decisions, as citizens, about the education of children.

■ Build self-esteem and self-confidence through successful and important work.

In your role as a coordinator, you will need to assess the goals of the tutoring program as identified by the school or agency. These goals may involve a wide range of language and literacy experiences, incorporating all ten ways literacy volunteers can help children described in Chapter 2 of this guide and in *Help America Read*.

Talk with people in the school or agency to identify needs. You might consider creating a written survey that you ask volunteers to complete. (See Appendix E.)

An agency or school may identify a few specific areas from the ten ways of working with children that they think are most important. For example, the school faculty may identify reading aloud to children as its primary need. Or, a teacher may prefer that volunteers focus on assisting children with writing skills. You'll want to design a training program that enables volunteers to develop the range of skills they will need to meet the identified needs in the setting where they work.

Making Time Work

Look at the time that your volunteers are able to give. Consider the amount of time available for service to children. You can then select the number of hours and variety of activities that volunteers can provide and use that information as a basis for planning the schedule for service and your training program. If training time is very limited, you might want to select two or three priorities (as identified by the staff in the school or community center) and provide an orientation and some initial training so that volunteers can begin to work. Later, you may involve them in further training.

The time involved in volunteer programs varies widely. Here are some examples.

■ A local college or university is participating in America Reads. They place supervised students in schools or community agencies for ten to twenty hours per week. Students receive "work study" stipends.

■ A local college or university has students who volunteer time (about five hours per week) to help children as part of a service learning curriculum.

■ A parent volunteer program has been established in the school. Some parents volunteer an hour per week but a small number can contribute up to five hours per week.

■ After-school learning centers have been organized to help children with homework and generally extend their learning. The centers are open from 3:00 to 6:00 p.m. Some are located in schools; others are in nearby churches, synagogues, boys' and girls' clubs, shelters, and other community centers. High-school students, college students, parents, and other citizens volunteer time in the after-school learning centers, usually about one afternoon per week.

■ A large church in an urban community has organized a Saturday daycare and learning center where children can stay from 8:00 a.m. to 4:00 p.m. Children ages three to twelve are eligible to attend. Community members volunteer time, usually about one Saturday per month.

■ A local synagogue provides a Sunday tutoring center from 1:30 to 5:00 p.m.

■ Senior citizens in an urban area are organized to work consistently in local schools, volunteering one to two hours per day to tutor specific children.

■ A local business has agreed to release its employees one to two hours in a work week to provide literacy tutorial services to children.

■ The National Service Corporation places members in local schools. They work daily with children for two to three hours, providing tutorial services in literacy.

With the variety of services and time available, the organizer of a volunteer program must be flexible. In this chapter, we have given you some suggestions for varying roles and training. Although we focus on the work that volunteers will do providing service directly to children, there are other roles, like helping with cafeteria and play time. While certainly valuable, these roles will not be addressed in this guide; our focus is on training volunteers to support early literacy. In the next chapter we will present a plan for a three-hour single training session. We'll also show you how to organize training to help volunteers use the ten ways of helping children learn to read and write in a direct and explicit manner.

Creating a High-Quality Training Program

Once you have made some decisions about the role volunteers will play in your setting, you are ready to decide how much training is needed and begin planning specific training sessions. A general principle is that the more training volunteers have (provided the training is of high-quality), the more effective they will be. Ongoing training is essential.

General Suggestions for Providing Quality Training

■ Conduct the training, if possible, at the place where volunteers will be serving children. This way, you'll have access to children for practice and the volunteers can become acquainted with the place and the staff. (Later, after volunteers get started, you may want to schedule another meeting or training session at a place away from the service setting.)

■ Plan about one to three hours for each training session. With less time, it is difficult to cover the material in depth. And without a comprehensive understanding of their work, volunteers will not feel fully confident as they begin tutoring children. What's more, short sessions do not leave time for

the questions and discussion that support learning. Long, intensive sessions may be difficult to schedule and also may cover too much material to be effective. If you must schedule a longer session, plan a short break.

■ Make the training fit volunteers' schedules as much as possible. Volunteers usually have limited time, so it must be time well spent.

■ Focus early training sessions on the specific activities that volunteers will do with children. For volunteers who are providing a variety of services (for example, reading to one or two children and then helping a child with writing), design separate training sessions for each literacy task, building the volunteers' literacy repertoire over time.

■ Include demonstration and practice with children in training sessions. A role-play situation or a short video clip can be very effective. Avoid long presentations and lectures.

■ Provide clearly written support materials.

■ Acquire the basic equipment and materials you need for training sessions; this includes an overhead projector and screen, a videotape player, chart paper and an easel, and markers and tape for hanging charts on the walls.

■ Provide for each participant 1) a copy of *Help America Read: A Handbook for Volunteers*; 2) a notebook for recording his or her observations of children and notes about tutoring; 3) a folder or notebook for keeping handouts and information on the setting for service. If you can, provide a volunteer "tool kit" (see Chapter 12 of *Help America Read*) for each person, or provide a larger "tool kit" that the volunteers share.

■ Make the tutoring materials available at the training sessions so that volunteer trainees can examine and handle them while learning their jobs.

■ Move each training session along at a lively pace. Start on time and end on time. Invite participants to ask questions and share their ideas, but try not to bog down in lengthy discussions. If you rarely accomplish the goals of the training sessions, neither you nor the participants will be satisfied.

General Processes for Training

In the appendixes for this guide, we have provided very specific plans, ranging from a single training session of three hours to a series of twelve two- to three-hour sessions that make up a year-long training course. You may select from these plans and adjust them to your own situation. Or, you might want to select any of the ten ways of working with children and plan your own sessions using *Help America Read* as a resource. As you plan your service training, you'll want to consider the unique needs and interests of your own group of volunteers and place of service, and adapt our guidelines to suit your purposes.

You may have just a few volunteers whom you are training right in the setting for service. In this case, you may simply want to follow some general principles for showing volunteers how to work with children. Invite the volunteers to try specific strategies and coach them until they feel comfortable. You'll see below a general framework we've outlined for working with volunteers in this way. You can use the framework to design volunteer training sessions on any topic. The series of actions might be accomplished in one session or two, depending on your situation.

Prepare

Practice the skill with children first so that you feel comfortable teaching it to others. Review and read appropriate parts of *Help America Read*.

Set up

Before the workshop, organize training materials and be sure that the place where you are meeting is neat and welcoming. Create an attractive display of children's books. Consider posting pictures of children to enhance your positive atmosphere. Make name tags if volunteers do not know each other.

Introduce the session

The introduction to the session will be brief but important. Introduce yourself and everyone to each other. Refreshments will help to "break the ice." Find a way to recognize the knowledge and skills that the volunteers bring to their work. Some may have had extensive experience working with children. Others may have valuable experiences (such as parenting, camp counseling, coaching, or scout leadership) but not realize how much of their knowledge will be useful in this new setting. Provide a brief introduction to the topic of the day. Include a brief rationale and description. Avoid a long presentation. Participants will learn more about the nature of the task and the potential values as they observe and experience it with children.

Demonstrate

Demonstrate with a child the skill you are introducing. Modeling the skill is much more effective than describing it at length. If you are working in a situation where children are available, you can demonstrate easily. Simply ask a child to work with you for a few minutes to show the volunteers how you engage children in reading or writing together. Have the volunteers sit in a circle and observe the activity for about fifteen minutes. They should remain silent but can take notes for later discussion and questions. If children are not available during the training, you can use a short videotape of yourself working with a child in the particular activity. Videotapes are not as useful as live demonstrations in the first training session, but as volunteers become more knowledgeable, videos can be effective. Videos should be about five to fifteen minutes in length. In our experience, participants get very little out of longer tapes, especially if the videos show people they do not know.

Discuss and reflect

Invite volunteers to discuss the demonstration they observed and to ask questions.

Repeat demonstration

Repeat the demonstration with another child and discuss it. This second demonstration will illustrate how the adult must adjust to each child. Two readings of the same book to two different children will vary because the adult responds to what each child notices and says.

Try it out

Divide volunteers into pairs and ask them to practice the skill with children. One volunteer observes while the other works with a child; then they change places and work with another child. Making this practice possible requires a large space (so that pairs can work at separate tables) and someone to bring children back and forth between tables. Remember that children are not wasting their time; they are profiting from interaction with adults. We suggest that the first time you invite volunteers to work in this way, try to keep the children and volunteers together. You'll want to spend your time walking around, observing volunteers,

detecting problems, and making suggestions or coaching in a way that will help each volunteer experience success from the beginning.

Reflect and analyze

Invite volunteer participants to reflect on their experience. They'll enjoy and benefit from their opportunities to observe each other at work on specific skills with children. Freed from interacting, the observer will have much more information about what happened during the session. Keep the discussion upbeat and positive. The purpose of the reflective discussion is not to critique; it is to sharpen observational power and, at the same time, develop the skills. Another purpose is to identify children's strengths.

Ask observers to address issues such as:

▮ What did the child respond to or notice?
▮ What could you tell that the child knew?
▮ How did the adult help the child?
▮ How could you tell the adult and child were enjoying themselves?

Read

Give participants a short, specific piece of written material that they can take home to read. You can use sections of *Help America Read* effectively in this way rather than asking volunteers to read the book from beginning to end.

Continue practice

If you time the training so that volunteers use their new skills with children the very next day, they will make the best use of their new knowledge. They will learn much more in the process.

Follow up

Hold a follow-up meeting to discuss volunteers' continued work with children. Hold this meeting after the volunteers have had a few days to try out their new skills. Once they've actually worked with children, they will have many questions and lots of information to discuss with their fellow volunteers.

▌ Start with success stories.

▌ Invite questions.

▌ Ask them to share problems (help them understand that problems are to be expected and that all will benefit from a frank discussion).

▌ Demonstrate again if needed.

If your time permits, offer to visit volunteers on-site while they work with children. Not everyone will feel comfortable with this, so make these visits optional. Ask if volunteers are finding their materials adequate and appropriate. Solve problems as needed.

Plan for a Single Session Training Program

The training needed to prepare volunteers for tutoring in each of the ten ways will vary according to the time available. The volunteer who is offering one hour a week will not expect more than a couple of hours of training, whereas the volunteer college student will probably devote more time to tutoring and will appreciate and need more training.

You may need to rely on a single initial training session to get volunteers started. A single session training program is presented in Appendix A. The single session plan calls for two to three hours of training and includes the orientation. Adjust the plan according to your needs and the time available. If you are able to hold the orientation at a different time, you can spend more time on reading aloud—even letting the volunteers try it out with children. We believe that this plan is minimal and that a truly effective volunteer program requires much more training. Consider this a beginning and plan to provide more training, if possible, during the period of service.

This initial training will prepare literacy volunteers to read to children and to write for them when necessary. For volunteers who tutor one hour per week, these two activities are a good beginning. Later, if the

volunteers want to try a new task, plan an additional one-hour training session.

Plan a Series of Training Sessions

Next, we describe ways to organize a more comprehensive training series. In Appendix A, we also present twelve sample plans from which to select. Using all of these plans provides twenty-four to thirty-six hours of training, spaced over time. We have planned twelve two-hour sessions; however, you could extend them to three hours (or two separate one and one-half hour sessions) by including more demonstration and discussion. You can follow up each session after a few days or a week with a sharing session in which volunteers discuss their own work with children. Extending the time and inviting participants to talk about their work with children will greatly enhance the experience for them and deepen their learning.

Use the Session Plans

These session plans are detailed and include useful activities. Here are some suggestions for making them your own.

▌ Adjust these activities to your own time and needs.

▌ Combine sessions or break them up into shorter segments.

▌ Use the sessions in any order (although the order we outline here represents the order of chapters in *Help America Read*).

▌ Use *Help America Read* as a constant resource.

▌ At the beginning of each session invite participants to quickly review the chart of ten ways literacy volunteers can help children so they will understand how each activity fits into an overall program of activities.

▌ Always bring closure to each session. Let participants ask questions, make comments about new learning or understandings, bring up examples from their own lives, and so forth. In our plans we use the term "questions and comments" to indicate closure at the end of each session. The process will help you to evaluate the session and its value for participants.

▮ Take a few minutes at the end of each session to write a few notes evaluating the session. Think about what was successful as well as additional points you want to develop with participants.

▮ The transparencies included in Appendix B are coordinated with each plan. You can use these transparencies on an overhead projector and/or as handouts on which participants can write notes for themselves.

▮ Consider one or two follow-up sessions for each of the twelve plans. When participants try out the particular activity, collect their own examples and share them with the group. As they share their experiences, they deepen their understanding and extend their learning.

Create a Course Structure

If you are working in a college or university setting, the series of sessions provides enough contact time for a three-credit-hour course (according to the quarter system). We strongly recommend extending training through observation and coaching while volunteers are working with children. With the follow-up sessions we suggest, this practicum time can also be part of the course, making it possible to do a three-credit-hour course in a semester system.

A general structure is used for each of the twelve series plans in Appendix A. Each plan includes:

▮ *Time:* A suggested time block for the activity.

▮ *Goals:* Primary accomplishments for the session in terms of participants' learning.

▮ *Preparing for the session:* Tasks you will want to do before the session.

▮ *Materials:* Materials you will want to gather and organize before the session.

▮ *Schedule:* A suggested schedule of activities—the detailed process for the training session. This includes explanations, directions, references to transparencies for making key points or engaging the participants in interactions, and references to figures and information in the handbook.

▮ *Questions and comments:* A suggested time for participants to ask questions, make comments, and share new insights.

▮ *Follow-up sessions:* A list of suggestions for planning follow-up sessions in the particular area.

▮ *Evaluating the session:* Space for you to jot down notes evaluating the session.

Organize for Coordinating and Training

The primary materials for the training course are the handbook, this guide, and a collection of sample plans. We recommend organizing your training materials into a three-ring notebook with these sections:

▮ *Volunteer information.* Create a list of the volunteers' names, addresses, and telephone numbers (work and home when appropriate). Also include information on their schedules and placement for service. It will help to keep notices and announcements in the notebook to use again or to provide models.

▮ *Information on the setting for service.* Include vital information about the setting for service—location, rules and procedures, supervisors, contact people, and so forth. If you are working in a school, include a list of all staff members with whom volunteers are working as well as a map of the building.

▮ *Surveys.* Make photocopied masters of information surveys that you plan to use and include them in the notebook so you can reproduce them when needed.

▌ *Session plans.* You may want to reproduce the session plans and put them in a binder. There is white space in the margins for you to make your own notes.

▌ *Transparencies.* You can photocopy the transparency masters in Appendix B. You can also use them as handouts on which the participants record their notes. Include both masters and transparencies in your notebook.

▌ *Examples to use in training sessions.* As you work with children, you may collect

interesting stories or samples of children's work. Include these in your notebook because they make good extensions for the session plans.

Use Your Time

As a literacy volunteer coordinator, your time is valuable. Being organized will help you use your time wisely. You will also serve as an inspiring model for your volunteers. High-quality training is essential for an effective program. Planning and organization are the keys to good training.

Reaching Out to Families

With our changing and highly mobile society, it is more important than ever to build strong connections between schools, families, and other organizations that support our citizens. Sixty percent of families with school-age children are headed by a single parent. In most cases, both parents in two-parent families must work outside the home in order to meet the cost of living demands. Parents and guardians have less time than ever to help children with reading and writing. Many lack both the resources and the information to effectively help their children into literacy. Television widens children's experience but does not help them much in the beginning stages of learning to read and write. Computers provide important experiences, but for beginning readers there are no substitutes for books, pencils or markers, and paper. Children need to find out what print is all about—how it can be enjoyed and how it can be produced for different purposes.

Volunteers who work in organizations other than schools (for example, community centers and churches) can play an important role in home literacy and can help to create three-way partnerships among the schools, homes, and organizations where they work.

In Chapter 11 of *Help America Read*, we list some simple ways that individual volunteers can reach out to children's families.

As a leader of volunteers, you can organize projects in your setting; for example:

■ A reading room where parents can find reading materials on child care and education.

■ A check-out library of good books that parents can read to their children at home.

■ A "homework hot line" that parents and children can call for assistance.

■ A system for "publishing" the books that children write, and displaying them in small libraries or special collections.

■ A home book program that will provide books for children and families to create a permanent collection at home.

■ A program to assure that children have writing materials in their homes.

■ Child care for younger children when parents attend workshops or meetings.

■ Workshops on book making so that parents can enjoy making books at home with their children.

In this guide, we describe in detail several activities that you, as the volunteer coordinator, may want to use to enhance the literacy effort in your school, church, or community center. These activities have all been tried and were successful in a variety of schools—urban, suburban, and rural. All require good organization and planning, but, once in place, volunteers can easily manage them.

Creating a Writing Case for Home Literacy

Not only is it important for children to read at home, they also need chances to write. Parents may not fully understand how children benefit from experimenting with writing. They may think that pencils are dangerous in the hands of young children or that children should simply copy correct material. They may think that children should not write until they can do so perfectly.

The writing case is a way to help parents appreciate the efforts their young children make as new writers. They can write something—their names or a few letters representing a message. The case brings writing into the home and enables caregivers to enjoy helping their children learn more about writing.

What is the writing case?

The writing case is a small plastic briefcase, file case, or large lunch box that has a handle and is easy for a young child to carry. Inside the case are writing materials that are easy to obtain and that children often see people using. Volunteers might include:

- Sheets of blank paper—half sizes and full sizes—of different colors.
- Small, spiral-bound notebooks.
- Blank paper folded to make books.
- Blank paper stapled together in book form.
- An alphabet chart.
- Stick-on notes.
- Any other kind of paper that is available.
- Envelopes of any kind.
- Pencils.
- Crayons.

- Colored markers (washable).
- Small ruler.
- Child-size scissors.
- Glue stick.
- Small stapler.
- Hole puncher and brads.
- A letter to parents explaining how to use the writing case (see Appendix D).

It is a good idea to include supplies that are easily obtainable at little or no cost and are often already around the house. The blank backs of envelopes, for example, are great for young children to use for writing. Businesses may be willing to donate some of these materials for the project. Caregivers do not need to spend money to provide writing opportunities for their children, they just need to know how important it is.

Introducing the writing case to children

Be sure to explain to the volunteers that they should introduce each child to the writing case. They should help the children understand how special it is and explain that each will have a chance to take it home. Help the volunteers follow these guidelines:

- Show each child—individually or as a group—all of the materials, letting each child handle them.

- Demonstrate how to: choose materials, think of something to write, write something, and return it to the case to bring back.

- Let a child demonstrate the process.

- Allow one child to take home the case for one night. (Try to talk with the child's parent beforehand about the project, and include a letter of explanation [see Appendix D]. You might also consider a home visit that will support the project. If you are working in a school, check with the teacher and principal before making a home visit.)

- The next morning invite the child to show you and the group his or her writing.

❚ Praise the child for taking care of the materials.

❚ Invite another child to take the case for a night.

Organizing and managing the writing case
How often should children take home the writing case? That will vary according to the number of children involved and the extent of the volunteer's contact with children's families. Generally, once a week is enough. If several children are involved, each child may get to take the case home every two or three weeks. Volunteers may find that they need more than one case.

After the child who has taken the case home returns with his writing, remind the volunteer to find the time to share and celebrate the writing. If the child does not actually use the case or write at home, be sure the volunteer doesn't scold or criticize the child in any way. It may be that the adults in the child's home are too busy with the evening meal or with outside jobs to help the child at home. With more practice with the literacy volunteer, the child will learn to use the case on his own at home. Be sure the volunteer praises every effort.

Involving Parents and Other Caregivers

Communication with children's families will greatly increase the effectiveness of the writing case. As caregivers see their children's writing, they will discover many ways to praise and help them, so it is important to involve them as much as possible.

The writing case is only one way to expand writing in the home. Encourage volunteers to take every opportunity to communicate to parents the value of children's writing. For example, a short note thanking the parent for allowing the child to bring in a sample of writing completed at home will encourage more. Sometimes, just sending home one or two sheets of paper and a thin marker will help. You can ask businesses to donate in-dividual writing kits with just a few materials and refrigerator magnets that will encourage the children's families to display their writing. Our goal is to foster a love of writing in children. We want them to choose to write at home because they enjoy it and feel pride in their efforts.

Extending Home Writing and Reading

Consider helping volunteers establish a "Mr. or Ms. Bear" book bag or backpack for children to take home. If your volunteers are working in schools, you will want to meet with classroom teachers to explain this idea and show them how it works. Then, you should plan a training session for volunteers to prepare them for using Mr. Bear or another stuffed animal such as a dinosaur or book character.

The idea of "Mr. or Ms. Bear" is to have a lovable toy that children get to know and interact with using literacy as it travels back and forth from home to tutoring settings. The stuffed toy helps to make the literacy experiences special and important. It also helps the children remember their literacy tasks. And finally, working with a stuffed toy motivates them to bring their written products back to school. Here's how it works.

❚ Included in a backpack or bag is a letter to family members explaining the use of the backpack or bag, a stuffed animal, a journal for writing, and some books.

❚ The child who is designated to take "Mr. or Ms. Bear" is responsible for carrying the backpack home, reading books to the stuffed toy, and writing, with his family, something in the journal about the bear's experiences in the child's home. The child and his or her family can read all of the other "adventures" in the journal recorded when other children took home "Mr. or Ms. Bear."

❚ Parents are encouraged to support and help the child in writing and reading.

Typically, both the child and other family members write entries in the journal.

The "Mr. or Ms. Bear" backpack is easy to assemble. Ask for contributions from local businesses or from families whose children are older. They may have extra bags or backpacks. Ask for contributions of stuffed animals. Volunteers may work together to assemble several of these backpacks at one time and then introduce them into the place where they work with children. The KEEP BOOKS™, described later in the chapter, may also be used in "Mr. or Ms. Bear" backpacks.

A Program for Borrowing Books

Volunteers can help to expand home reading by managing a check-out program to provide literature for children to take home. Public libraries are, of course, an invaluable community resource and volunteers can greatly help to extend their value by assisting librarians, reading stories to children, and advising parents on books to take out. But supplemental lending programs are essential for increasing children's exposure to books for the following reasons. While it is true that most elementary schools have libraries, an individual child may spend time in the library only once a week. In addition, some schools do not allow kindergarten or first-grade children to check out books. Young children need to be close to books and explore books every day. Lending programs can be established anywhere—in churches, in classrooms, and in community centers.

Here are some principles volunteers should keep in mind as they establish a lending program.

∎ Since many of the beginning books are short, children need to take home more than one book at a time. Some of the books might be the kind of books they are reading in their school instruction and are not available in libraries.

∎ Even young children need the experience of caring for a book and returning it.

∎ Sending books home every day provides parents with the kind of material they need to read to their children without having to visit the library (whose hours may not be convenient for parents) or spend money to buy books.

∎ Children will enjoy taking some books home more than once, so that parents can repeat the reading of favorite books.

Public and school libraries already have well-developed systems for lending books. The lending system that volunteers set up in a classroom or community center is usually more flexible.

Acquiring a Book Collection

Assemble a collection of books. There may be books in the classroom library that children can use at school, but not take home. If volunteers are organizing the lending program, they should consider creating a special shelf or bin where they can store the group of lending books. That way, they'll avoid a mix-up. It is a good idea, though, to keep in the lending library duplicates of many of the books teachers and volunteers are reading aloud to children. Those are the books children will want to take home.

If funds are available, suggest to volunteers that they consider purchasing a quantity of books from a wholesale dealer. Because the collection will probably be limited, it is necessary to choose each selection carefully. At the end of *Help America Read*, volunteers will find a list of "books too good to miss" for grade levels K–3. These books have good stories and characters that appeal to children. After reading through many of these books, volunteers will find that a trip to the bookstore will turn up many more. Avoid buying collections without actually seeing the books first. Volunteers should start with a smaller number and watch to see which books children request repeatedly, and then buy multiple copies of those books. Sometimes local bookstores will contribute books. Businesses may sponsor a certain number of books each year.

Books are often less expensive when purchased from book clubs, and free books are sometimes available with the purchase of a quantity of books. It is nice to have hardback books and they do last longer; however, many books are available in high-quality paperback. In Chapter 11 of the handbook, we have included the names and address of two good book clubs.

Using the collection
As volunteers help to create a lending library, they'll want to:

▌ Find ways to preserve books so that the collection will last a long time.

▌ Cover books with plastic for durability; we recommend plastic because it repels dirt and keeps books from tearing. Plastic covers may be purchased for all sizes of children's books. You can laminate the covers of paperback books.

▌ Give each child a clear plastic storage bag in which to take books home. We have found that putting the books in these bags (on which the child's name is printed in marker or on tape) not only preserves them but communicates to the child and family that the book is something special. And it increases the likelihood that the child will return the book the next day.

▌ Form a routine for taking a book home each day. It is hard for young children to remember that a book is "due" in a week. The daily taking home and bringing back of books builds good habits. Besides, all of the books that kindergarten, first-, and second-grade students take home can be read in one evening. If second- and third-graders are reading longer books, it makes sense to have a longer borrowing time; those children will have already learned the routine.

▌ Assemble enough books so that everyone who wants to can take a book home. If a very limited selection of books is available, children can take turns. Half the group can take home a book Monday and Tuesday, for example, and the other half can take home a book on Wednesday and Thursday.

▌ Help each child select a new book as soon as he or she returns a book in the morning. The book brought home the previous evening can be taken out of the plastic bag and a new one inserted, ready to bring home that afternoon. Browsing to select a new book is a good activity for children as they enter the room, and the literacy volunteer can easily manage this activity.

Teaching children to use the collection
By using a lending library, children bring literacy materials into their homes, enhancing the quality of their home life. It is also apparent that they are developing valuable skills. For example, a child is:

▌ Taking responsibility for something borrowed—taking it home and bringing it back.

▌ Helping to keep a collection in order.

▌ Taking care of a book each night.

▌ Building knowledge of books that they can share with friends and families.

▌ Contributing to the life of the family.

Learning to use the lending library collection will not happen automatically. The volunteer, with the help of the teacher, must teach children the necessary routines. Our lives are organized through routines: we have mealtime and bedtime routines that we follow almost every day; all of us know the rules of how to act in school, at a sporting activity, or in the grocery store. Children must be taught explicitly how to use the lending library collection. For example,

▌ We choose books within the time allowed.

▌ We put our books in the plastic bag.

■ At the end of the day, we take our books home.

■ At home, we look at the book, ask a family member to read it or look at it with us, put it back in the bag, and place it where we will remember it in the morning.

■ In the morning, we return the book and exchange it for another.

This simple routine is one that even very young children can remember. With the teacher's assistance, the volunteer can help children act out the routine, reteaching it as much as necessary until they understand their important roles. The learning that occurs when children know and use this routine will be useful to them throughout their school careers. It will help them know how to remember library books, textbooks, and homework.

A Home Book Program to "Keep"

It is widely known that efforts to teach reading are much more effective when children have books in their homes. Yet, the cost of books coupled with an adult's lack of time make it difficult for many caregivers to provide a large collection of books at home. Also, even though children may have some books that adults can read to them, it is unusual for the youngest children—those just starting to read—to have very many books at home that they can read for themselves.

The staff at Ohio State University designed a home book program, called KEEP BOOKS, that would give young children many more books at home and build a bridge between home and school. These books do not take the place of the quality children's literature that the library system must provide, but they are a way to increase children's home reading. The books are designed for school district or business donors and philanthropists to give away to children. For example, a local business provided a large number of KEEP BOOKS in an urban school district. The volunteers then placed a small sticker on each book identifying the business contributing the books. The not-for-profit KEEP BOOKS represent a low-cost way for districts to provide many home books.

An organization can create its own program of inexpensive books to keep by writing and illustrating a series of small books. The topic of books may focus on local people or places. After books are created, volunteers can help to reproduce and assemble them. Then, the program can be implemented following the guidelines for KEEP BOOKS presented in the next section. We caution that it is necessary to test any locally written books with children for ease of reading and interest before investing a great many resources in printing and distributing them.

What are KEEP BOOKS?

KEEP BOOKS are short, paperback books with simple stories and bright colors. They are sized to fit in a shoe box. The black and white drawings inside give children a clue to the meaning of the story. The drawings are produced by professional artists and evaluated for the way they help children in reading. A review process assesses KEEP BOOKS for their text quality and potential for supporting beginning reading strategies. Directions to children (and the front cover design) indicate that this is a different kind of book. Children discover that they can color or add to the pictures with markers or crayons and write their names (and sometimes their own text) in the books.

KEEP BOOKS focus on topics familiar to young children and encourage them to read and reread; however, parents and older siblings may also read these books aloud to children. Children are encouraged to put their names in these books and to keep them as a collection in a safe place (like a special box that they have decorated). The purpose of a home book program is to help children learn to be collectors of books and to preserve and use books in the home.

Creating and Managing a Home Book Program for Children

Volunteers can make a real contribution to early literacy by managing a home book program. They can administer the program from a church, a social agency, a hospital, or a school—anywhere children regularly come and can receive a book. Other books, besides the Ohio State University collection, can also be part of a take-a-book-home-to-keep program.

The easiest KEEP BOOKS have one line of text on each page and they increase in difficulty through eight sets. The hardest ones are approximately beginning second-grade level. They are provided by Ohio State on a not-for-profit basis at a low cost of 25 cents per book. (For more information, contact The Ohio State University Early Literacy Learning Initiative at 614-688-5770.) If you are creating your own home books, a good guideline is to provide between eight and twenty-four titles for each grade level—kindergarten and first grade. The program can cover several weeks, with books to take home each week. Children should establish a little reading box (such as the shoe box) in which they can keep other books as well as the books they create themselves with literacy volunteers.

It will not take much time to use these books as a regular part of children's experiences in the classroom or other tutoring setting. The literacy volunteer will introduce children to the books, teach them how to use the books, and then distribute the books.

It's a good idea to send home two letters to families about the program. One letter will alert them that volunteers are beginning the program. Families will need to send in a shoe box or other box that their child can use to store their books. Send the second letter when the child takes home her first books.

Explain to the volunteers that when they first introduce the home book program to the child or children they are working with, they might start by saying, "Today you are going to get a different kind of book, one that you can take home and keep. I'm going to show you how to take care of your books." Then, they can show the children their special book boxes and invite them to write their names on the boxes and decorate them in some way.

Volunteers will introduce the first book, using the format suggested below, and enjoy the book with the children. Then, they show the children how to put the books in their boxes and place their boxes in a safe place.

Caution the volunteers not to let the children take home their boxes and the first books immediately, because they will want to help the children practice taking out the books, rereading them, and putting them away. If children come to the same place each day (such as a school or daycare center), volunteers can use the box at school for the first five to ten books. This experience teaches children an important responsibility: how to save and take care of books. They also acquire good reading practice.

Sometimes volunteers like to keep the book box at the school or center for a longer period of time and then, eventually, send it home. This practice allows for rereading the books as part of the volunteers' work with children. Other volunteers have one set of books that they use for rereading with the child. For example, the volunteer could have one decorated box that stays in the place where children are served. Children would be able to use the collection to select and read books. Another set goes home, so that the child can see the same literacy materials and use the same techniques in both places.

Help volunteers practice introducing the books to children. First, volunteers can try some of the following steps.

■ Have a brief conversation with the child (or a small group of children) showing enthusiasm and building interest in the book. Describe what the book is about.

▌ Leaf through the pictures and discuss what is happening in each picture.

▌ Use some of the language of the story as you discuss it with the children. Volunteers can read the book to very young children, or if the children are already able to read a little, the volunteer might repeat some of the language of the story without reading the whole book. For example, the adult might say, "In this story, the baby cried and cried."

▌ If the text is easy, the children should read it, using the suggestions in Chapter 7 of *Help America Read*. If it is a little harder, use the book for shared reading, as in Chapter 6.

▌ Each new day that a volunteer works with the books, he or she should reread those that were introduced earlier.

Extending KEEP BOOKS

Children may use the KEEP BOOKS as models for making their own books or for their own writing. Occasionally, if appropriate, volunteers may relate books to particular activities; for example, as children read the book *Making a Peanut Butter and Jelly Sandwich*, they could actually make a sandwich and then read the book again. Children can make their own books about the sandwich (making it more personal by writing their own name into the story, explaining what kind of jelly they used, etc.).

Involving Parents and Other Caregivers

Remind volunteers of the importance of helping parents and other caregivers understand the home book program. Help them discover how to use the books with their children. Volunteers can reach caregivers through

▌ Parent workshops at times and locations convenient for them.
▌ Handwritten notes or letters.
▌ Telephone calls.
▌ Home visits.

Involving Families

Help volunteers understand the special role they can play in reaching out to children's families. Sometimes, this is the best way volunteers can contribute especially if they are working in a school where teachers and others are concentrating time and attention on instruction.

Good collaboration and communication with the staff will enable volunteers to organize and provide many materials and plans that will involve children's families in literacy learning. The teamwork among parents and other caregivers, the community, and the educational personnel create ideal learning conditions and benefit children immeasurably.

Troubleshooting

Nothing worth doing is easy. When you coordinate a volunteer literacy program, it is best to anticipate potential problems and have systems in place to deal with them. In this chapter, we address five problems that arise frequently when volunteers are working with children.

You may be connected with a university or business that is organizing volunteers. Or, you may be on the receiving end, trying to organize groups of volunteers who are offered to your school, center, or church. Whatever the situation, the leaders and coordinators will want to work closely with each other to discuss problems and make decisions. If you are working in a school and are organizing volunteers from a large, local corporation that has "adopted" the school, establish one contact person from the business with whom you can talk frequently about the volunteers' training and service. Many universities are sending out college students through America Reads; programs like City Year and AmeriCorps have many volunteers in schools. Each has an administrative structure in place for troubleshooting.

Absenteeism

For the enthusiastic volunteer, it is disappointing to arrive again and again at the place of service and find that a child is absent. Even the most committed volunteers can begin to doubt their effectiveness. Here are some suggestions to help you, as the leader of volunteers, cope with the absentee problem.

■ Set up a communication system to check attendance every morning. In a school or daycare center, teachers can post the names of absent children right on the classroom door where you can see them. You can also report names to a central location by sending a note or using the intercom.

■ Post the names and telephone numbers of volunteers (and the children they serve) in the office. Ask a staff member to call a volunteer if his or her student is absent.

■ Give one volunteer the task of checking absences and calling other volunteers when necessary. This job diversification might suit the schedule of one of your volunteers.

■ Some children are chronically absent, posing a particular problem for the volunteer program. Because they miss so much school, these children are often the very ones who need the extra help volunteers can give, so you do not want to remove them from the list of children who receive benefits. At the same time, it is very frustrating for the volunteer to try to work with such a child. Here are some tips for this particular situation.

∎ The volunteer who is reading to children and involving them in shared reading can easily work with two children at once. Thus, on days when a child is absent, that volunteer will simply work with only one child.

∎ Volunteers who work with children individually may be serving one or more children in sequence. Continue to allow the volunteer to serve the frequently absent child, but set up an arrangement with another child as an alternate. So, on any given day, a volunteer who has time to work with two children in turn will have a pool of three children. The volunteer always has someone to see.

∎ There are service settings in which the group of children can be unstable, for example, in homeless shelters and temporary housing. In this case, concentrate on the service to be performed without assigning particular children to each volunteer. Volunteers simply come to the setting at a particular time and work with whomever is there. Over time, they will get to know some of the children well, although intensive tutoring relationships might be hard to develop. Although this situation is less than ideal, we believe it is better than offering no service at all.

Time Commitment Problems

Sometimes volunteers want to make the commitment to service but, after they get

started, find that they really do not have the time. Or, a volunteer may be required by law or school curriculum to participate in service—and thus lacks enthusiasm for the job. Whatever the reason, be prepared to have some volunteers who are irregular in attendance or who are consistently late. Here are some suggestions for coping with the situation.

∎ Monitor attendance and promptness closely for the first few weeks of the volunteer program. This close monitoring will be helpful to volunteers as they begin their service, because you will be able to answer questions and offer some informal training. If you work outside the volunteer setting, your consistent presence from the beginning will help you get to know key staff members and set up monitoring systems like those described for children's absence.

∎ Provide a phone number that volunteers can call if they are ill or an emergency arises and they must be absent or late.

∎ Work individually with volunteers who are showing signs of being undependable. Help them evaluate their schedules. Schedules in a volunteer program are generally flexible. As long as the service with the child fits into the school or center schedule, time can be adjusted to meet the needs of volunteers. You can

∎ Find a better time for a volunteer who is having difficulty arriving promptly.

∎ Help the volunteer solve problems related to transportation or baby-sitting.

∎ Reduce the amount of time a volunteer is committing.

∎ Adjust the schedule to find days that are more convenient for the volunteer.

∎ Delay the start of the volunteer's service until he or she can make schedule adjustments.

∎ Counsel volunteers on the nature of the service they have selected. Perhaps they are not comfortable with the work. Again, it is easy to make adjustments. There are many different tasks that volunteers can choose to perform. For example, volunteers who are not enjoying their work with children can give service by gathering and organizing materials.

∎ The setting may not be convenient for the volunteer; for example, if commuting time far exceeds service time, the setting may be too far away for the volunteer. In this case, you may want to recommend a different program in a more convenient location.

Events That Interfere with Tutoring

If volunteers arrive at the place of service and find that children are unavailable because of other events that are scheduled, they are likely to become frustrated and discouraged.

∎ Set up a calendar for the year that clearly identifies major events and holidays. Check the calendar each month for changes and provide an update for volunteers. (Again, this could be a task delegated to a dependable volunteer.)

∎ Provide volunteers with written directions on school-closing procedure for inclement weather (which radio station or television station to tune to, for example).

∎ Set up a telephone "chain" that will allow the group of volunteers to contact each other quickly if children will be unavailable because of schedule changes or weather.

∎ Provide a phone number that volunteers can call for information if they are uncertain whether the school or agency will be open on a given day.

∎ Check the calendar for the coming month each time you meet with volunteers. Prompt them to ask teachers or staff members if any special events are coming up.

∎ Establish a "fall-back" task for the volunteer who does show up and has nothing to do because of special events or children's absence. For example, the volunteer might spend some time organizing new materials or making blank books for writing.

Tutoring Problems

Volunteers, especially those who are inexperienced, may need extra support to be successful in their work with children. There are two common problems:

∎ The volunteer has difficulty managing the task assigned.
∎ The volunteer has difficulty managing children's behavior.

If the first problem arises, remember that some of the ten ways of working with children may be entirely new to one or more of your volunteers. It may take some time to understand

∎ The nature of the task.
∎ Why the task is important.
∎ All the necessary steps.
∎ How to engage children and capture their attention.
∎ How to vary the task in response to different children.
∎ How to change the task over time to meet children's needs as they learn more.
∎ How to relax and enjoy interacting with children while working on the task.

A volunteer may become discouraged and appeal to you for help; or, the volunteer may not realize that things are going wrong. In either case, here are some ideas that may help.

∎ Reteach the task to the volunteer individually. Working with one person instead of a group is often helpful because he or she can ask specific questions.

▌ Demonstrate the task to the volunteer and then ask him or her to try it. Coach the volunteer through the task as many times as necessary. Sometimes it helps to observe the interaction, coach, and then ask the volunteer to repeat the task right away, focusing on just one or two changes.

▌ Help the volunteer organize materials so that it is easier to keep the task going.

▌ Videotape the volunteer while he or she works with a child. Then watch the videotape together, acknowledging when the work is going well and providing suggestions for improvement. This technique will help the volunteer build understanding of what the child is gaining from the activity.

▌ Always praise and encourage the volunteer for trying. Acknowledge that you know it is not easy to accomplish some of these complex tasks with young children. Reassure the volunteer that, with time, it will get much easier.

▌ In some cases, a task is just not right for a particular volunteer. An example might be someone who is self-conscious about reading aloud. In that case, simply change the volunteer's role. There is plenty of work to do in any setting devoted to literacy learning. It is possible to find something that is right for almost everyone.

The second problem, behavior management, raises new issues. Remember that volunteers are not the primary managers of the children's learning. They provide extra support. Their time with children must be enjoyable. If a volunteer is having difficulty managing children's behavior when working in a small group, simply advise that volunteer to work with children individually. If the same problems occur in the one-to-one setting, here are some suggestions.

▌ Model some ways of working with the child that will help the volunteer learn how to manage behavior—for example, giving explicit directions, being pleasant but firm, not allowing distraction, moving the pace along in the session, and so forth.

▌ Observe the volunteer working with the child and offer suggestions afterward (or coach her through the lesson).

▌ Ask the child's classroom teacher to advise the volunteer on how to work with the child.

▌ Help the volunteer understand how to make the session more engaging for the child (for example, the books the volunteer is choosing might be too difficult or uninteresting).

▌ Counsel the volunteer to be highly organized so that no "down" time is spent looking for materials—a distracting situation.

▌ Place the volunteer to work with another child, if all else fails with the first placement. There are many children who can profit from the service. It is not right to deny children service because of behavior that may be beyond their control, but sometimes a professional expert is needed rather than a volunteer. Work with the child yourself for a while, or try to find more appropriate help.

Volunteer and Personnel Conflicts

Whenever people work closely together, there are cooperative arrangements to make and, inevitably, problems to solve. For example, when a classroom teacher has one or more volunteers working in a classroom, that means several people must cooperate daily to share space and materials, modify the level of noise in their interactions, find times to communicate, and find ways to become colleagues and partners in the interest of children. Neither classroom teachers nor volunteers may realize how much adjustment it will take. Other settings, too, have primary purposes and staff members with whom the volunteers must interact. Here are some suggestions for preventing and resolving conflicts.

▌ Prevent problems, as much as possible, by using the suggestions in this guide for orientation and training.

▌ Meet for as long as necessary with staff and volunteers early in the implementation of the project. Time spent here will pay off in problem prevention.

▌ Be organized so that you can facilitate conflicts regarding schedules and materials.

▌ Communicate clearly in writing with everyone.

▌ Meet right away with everyone involved. If a conflict does arise, the key is not to let it continue. It is easier to solve a new problem than a long-standing one.

▌ Always try to see all perspectives in any conflict. It may seem that staff members are not accommodating enough to volunteers or demonstrating their appreciation for free help. From their point of view, however, the changes may not always be worth the help. It takes time for everyone to see the results of programs.

▌ Help people talk to each other instead of going through you or someone else. Being the "go between" may cause more misunderstandings.

▌ Have regular communication sessions and encourage people to take a problem-solving stance in these sessions. Reassure them that

problems are normal, and that it takes time to work out all arrangements.

▌ Meet in a special session with a pair or small group of people who are having difficulty. You may need to clear up misunderstandings about what volunteers do or the nature of the program. You may need to adjust schedules or change the volunteers' roles.

▌ If conflicts can not be overcome, change a volunteer's assignment. Volunteering should be rewarding, not stressful.

Keeping Your Perspective

Even though problems will arise in implementing a volunteer program, remember that you have many resources. Also remember that most volunteers will cheerfully and skillfully do their jobs with very little difficulty and most staff members will welcome them and bend over backward to assure the success of the program.

As you consider the problems that may arise, keep in mind that you are *not* solely responsible either for the program or for solving every single problem.

▌ Bring interested people from the staff and the agency together to work as a team.
▌ Ask for suggestions.
▌ Involve volunteers in leadership roles to prevent and solve problems.
▌ Create teams to support each other.
▌ Create your own supportive group that you can count on as a sounding board.

No problem is so great that it can not be solved if people keep their eyes on the goal—helping children become successful readers and writers.

Becoming a Leader

Organizing and leading a literacy volunteer program is a complex and demanding task. An obvious benefit of your role is the satisfaction you'll derive as you see both children and volunteers learning and enjoying their work together. Coordinating this worthwhile effort will also give you a chance to exercise your leadership skills and enjoy teaching adults.

In this final chapter we explore facets of leadership that will enable you to do a good job as a coordinator of volunteers and make your work manageable. Your coordinating role may be important, but part-time. You may coordinate literacy volunteers as part of another complex job. Consider your own time and capacities as you analyze your role as a literacy coordinator. No matter how effective the program is, it will not continue if the personnel can not manage it effectively. At all times, you need to keep in mind two goals:

■ Enhancing children's literacy achievement.
■ Managing the leadership role and your own time and responsibilities successfully.

Both are important if the program is to succeed and last.

Managing Training

In Chapter 1 we presented the research that describes the essentials of successful programs. Research indicates that good literacy volunteer programs are characterized by expert training and supervision of volunteers. The structure of this plan will provide a rich experience for your volunteers. The plan will be more effective, however, as you weave in your own insights and knowledge. To enhance your role as a trainer of literacy volunteers,

■ Practice every technique with children. Work as much as you can with children, using all of the approaches we recommend in this guide. The more experience you have, the more credibility you will have with the volunteers you prepare. Working with children will give you confidence; you will know the details of the task. Moreover, you will have real life experiences to relate to your trainees. Sometimes the most effective point you can make is to talk about a child with whom you are working.

■ Develop some of your own resources. A brief videotape of your own work with children will be very effective. You do not have to be perfect. In fact, explain to volunteers that you have reflected on the session and would do a few things differently. They'll find your honesty reassuring.

■ Continue to expand your knowledge and skills through your work with volunteers. Every time you observe and coach a volunteer, you will also learn something new.

■ Invite volunteers to share with each other. The more you can make your group interdependent rather than dependent on you for expertise, the more effectively they will work together. After all, as they gain expertise, they can help each other. And, experienced volunteers can help new ones. No single person can provide all the expertise that creates a highly successful program.

■ Be sure that volunteers know how to use the handbook, *Help America Read*. If you use this resource in training sessions and encourage volunteers to read and refer to it when they have questions about their work, they will become more knowledgeable and independent.

Supervising Literacy Volunteers

Supervision is another challenge for the leader of literacy volunteers. It may be difficult for you to direct or manage the activities of others. It is critical to establish a good relationship with the volunteers you supervise. Volunteers are not employees. Some may be there as part of a job or education-related requirement or they may have made a commitment to a program that pays a living stipend; these volunteers do have a formal obligation to the program. But, for the most part, if volunteers have a bad experience, they can simply walk away from their work.

If they do leave the program, however, they will not feel good about the outcome of the experience. They volunteered for a rea-son—to give service—and they have high expectations. They trust you to help them meet their goals and achieve the rewards of helping children. Thus, the trust you establish with the volunteers you supervise is very important. Your support, leadership, and management can make all the difference.

Ten Goals for Effective Management

Below we have listed ten characteristics of effective volunteer supervisors. These characteristics will play out in different ways in different settings, because we all have our own unique styles.

1. Be clear about expectations.
To be successful, volunteers must know what is expected of them. In the interviews, orientation, training sessions, and follow-up consultations, be specific in describing what volunteers are expected to do in your setting. Also, be clear about what they are *not* expected or even allowed to do. If there are misunderstandings, clear them up right away.

2. Be prompt, organized, dependable, and efficient.
If you expect volunteers to be dependable, you must be dependable yourself. Your actions in terms of being ready and on time for sessions and appointments speak louder than words. For example, begin and end training sessions precisely on time. This is especially important as you begin the program. If sessions start late, even those who originally were prompt will not bother to arrive on time. Your consideration of volunteers' time will show them how much you value their participation and will also send the message that time counts—for everyone involved in the program.

To achieve your goals of dependability and promptness, you will need to manage your own time efficiently. Like everyone else, you have personal responsibilities and, perhaps, other jobs. Analyze your time and determine how you can use it effectively.

3. Communicate often with everyone involved in the program.

Face-to-face communication is usually best. Just stopping by for a few minutes to see how things are going creates an atmosphere of easy give-and-take. You will learn much about volunteers' work, which will enable you to prevent problems. Conduct regular meetings to talk about the program; these gatherings do not have to be lengthy or formal. A quick brown-bag lunch can accomplish much in establishing an atmosphere of friendliness and trust. Written communications are also necessary, but remember that complex matters can not be handled effectively through memos. In general, people do not care to read and follow complex written directions. Oral communication is the key.

4. Be prompt in following through a plan of action.

All of us are busy. If we push tasks to the bottom of the list, we sometimes forget their importance. Schedule a time to accomplish the tasks you must complete.

5. Recognize volunteer efforts— successful and unsuccessful.

Everyone appreciates recognition. It is not necessary to praise people constantly, but it makes a positive difference to notice their work. The volunteers with whom you work will appreciate your comments. Compliment volunteers when you know the children with whom they have been working have made special progress. Or, mention how pleased a teacher is with their efforts. Many supervisors take the time to write brief notes or communicate on email when they see a volunteer exceeding expected time commitments or working in an especially effective way with a child. Remember, also, the impor-

tance of celebrations and culminating experiences. Organize a volunteer appreciation breakfast or lunch. At the end of a year of service provide a certificate of appreciation. (See a sample certificate in Appendix F). Encourage staff members in the service setting to appreciate the volunteers' efforts. Additionally, compliment the staff members and appreciate their efforts to be good hosts.

6. Be open to suggestions.

Look for input from the volunteers themselves and from others. The more information you have, the more effectively you can accomplish your job.

7. Be a good listener.

When people are meeting new challenges, they often need an opportunity to talk to someone. This may be true of the volunteers in your setting. You do not have to solve every problem, nor do you have to act or give direct advice. Sometimes it is enough just to listen. Moreover, listening carefully to what people say will sometimes help you in solving other problems. Treat every individual as someone who is giving you important information.

8. Establish a support system for yourself.

Find a person or a small group of people who are willing to talk with you about your work as a coordinator. At least one such person should be knowledgable about the program so that you can get another perspective on progress and problems. Ask your support people for honest feedback. A good support person will tell you the problems and help you address them without blaming you. Don't choose a volunteer as a confidante, even if the person is a friend. Your work with volunteers is confidential.

9. Share the sunshine.

As the old saying goes, "When the sun shines, it shines on everyone." There will be enough attention and rewards to go around as the literacy volunteer program becomes successful. Do not hesitate to give a large share of credit to everyone involved in creating this new venture. At celebration times, be sure that you recognize everyone.

10. Work with children yourself.

Your priority must always be children's learning. As much as possible, work with children yourself. As a coordinator, there will be days when you are bogged down in administrative detail. It is easy to become frustrated. But the moment you begin to work with a child who is delighted with her growing ability to read and write, everything will fall into place. Give yourself the gift of seeing children succeed. You will remember why you are doing what you are doing, and you will experience the rewards for yourself. This will give you the boost to complete your important work —helping literacy volunteers make a difference for children.

APPENDIXES

Orientation for Literacy Volunteers
Session Plan

1. Introduction of volunteers and staff members
Recognize each person. Invite the volunteers to talk briefly about themselves and share their reasons for volunteering. Introduce the staff members as well and invite them to welcome the volunteers and show their appreciation for the volunteers' service.

2. Overview of the program
Avoid giving a long presentation. You may want to provide a brief, ten- to fifteen-minute overview of the program, stressing the benefits to children and the importance of the services that volunteers will perform.

3. *Help America Read: A Handbook for Volunteers*
Distribute and briefly introduce the volunteers to *Help America Read: A Handbook for Volunteers*, explaining its use. Invite each volunteer to look through the book for a few minutes and explain that you will use this resource in their training and work all year.

4. Address a list of questions about the nuts and bolts of the program.

- Where will volunteers work? Show volunteers where they will work and briefly introduce ideas that will help them organize materials in the working space. It will help to have one work area completely set up as an example. You might want to create the "tool kit" described in *Help America Read* (Chapter 12) and demonstrate storage and use of materials.
- Who will they work with?
- When will the volunteers work?
- What kinds of materials will they use?
- Who are the important contact people in the building or organization?
- What communication systems are in place to help volunteers?
- What operational procedures are essential to know from the beginning (such as what to do when you are absent)?

Read Chapter 1 of *Help America Read* for additional tips.

5. Announce when and where the training will be held. (In some cases, training might follow the orientation.) Suggest that the volunteers read Chapter 1 of *Help America Read* before the first training session.

6. Provide a tour of the building.
The orientation session described above should take about one hour. Of course, this session does not include training, but it provides a strong beginning on a positive note, conveys the seriousness of the volunteer role, and lets volunteers know their work is greatly valued and appreciated. To guarantee the session's success:

- Provide some light refreshments at the beginning of the meeting. Make the room attractive, tidy, and welcoming.
- Have name tags and ask everyone to wear them (yourself, staff, and volunteers).
- If you are in a school, be sure the principal is available to welcome the volunteers; in other settings, ask the person in charge to handle the greetings.

- Have materials neatly organized and ready before the meeting starts so that you can welcome and interact with the new volunteers. This will help them feel important and show them that you are prepared.
- If possible, invite people who have previously volunteered in the setting. They can share their enthusiasm and answer questions.

7. Questions

Evaluate the session.

Orientation and Getting Started with Reading Aloud and Writing for Children

Time: Approximately 2 to 3 hours

Goals:

1. To prepare volunteers for their roles when time for service and training are limited.
2. To incorporate all necessary information into a single training session.
3. To introduce the volunteers to the setting for service and provide information about it.
4. To provide training in reading aloud and writing for children.

Preparing for the session:

1. Assemble the orientation packets.
2. Arrange for facilities and people.
3. Notify everyone.
4. Make transparencies.
5. Review chapters 1, 2, 3, 5, and 6 of *Help America Read*.
6. Gather samples of high-quality books to read aloud (use Appendix A: Books Too Good to Miss from *Help America Read*).

Materials needed for the session:

1. Plan for the Session (for coordinator's use)
2. Orientation Packet (see Chapter 3 of this Guide)
3. *Help America Read: A Handbook for Volunteers*
4. Transparency: Meeting the Child
5. A book to read aloud to the group and a child (use the same book for both)
6. Transparency: Reading Aloud to Children
7. Notebook for each participant
8. Selection of books to read aloud

Schedule

1. *Orientation* (60 minutes)

- Distribute Orientation Packet and *Help America Read*.
- Introduce volunteers and staff members.
- Provide a brief overview.
- Give information about the nuts and bolts of the program.
- Discuss location and schedule for training.
- Provide a tour of the building.

2. *Talking with children*

- Make three or four key points about how to meet the child.

USE TRANSPARENCY: MEETING THE CHILD

- Talk about each of the points briefly and then refer participants to pages 12–13 of Chapter 3 in *Help America Read*.
- Ask them to look at the list of suggestions on pages 12–13 of Chapter 3, "Finding Ways to Talk with Children."

3. Read a book

- Read a good, short book from the volunteers' collection and recommend that they use a book like this one to break the ice with the child.
- Tell volunteers that there are some sample books for them to look at after the session. Refer them to Appendix A: Books Too Good to Miss in *Help America Read*.

4. Reading aloud to children

- If possible, bring in a child and read the same book, sitting beside the child and demonstrating the process (see Chapter 4 in *Help America Read*).
- Ask the participants to comment on what they observed as you read to the child.
- Make several key points about reading aloud.

USE TRANSPARENCY: READING ALOUD TO CHILDREN

5. Writing for children

- Refer to page 58, "Writing for Children," in Chapter 9 of *Help America Read*.
- Remind participants that they will sometimes write for children. They should use the recommended print chart on page 47 in Chapter 8 of *Help America Read*, using upper- and lowercase letters in a standard way.
- Suggest that they photocopy the recommended print chart and tape it up in their work areas.
- Ask them to read page 58, "Writing for Children," in Chapter 9 of *Help America Read*.

6. Assessing your work with children

- Point out that each chapter ends with a list of questions that invites them to think about their work with children. Explain that having informal written records and also simple written plans for sessions will make them more effective.
- Encourage the volunteers to obtain a notebook for writing down observations and plans for sessions. If you have resources, it is best to give each volunteer a special notebook for this purpose.

7. Questions

After the session

- Be available for individuals to ask questions and discuss schedules.
- Let participants browse through the book samples.

Evaluate the session.

Plan for a Series: Training Session #1

GETTING STARTED

Time: Approximately 2 to 3 hours

Goals:

1. Orient volunteers to the setting and their work.
2. Introduce *Help America Read* and the organizing framework ("ten ways literacy volunteers can help children").
3. Introduce the tool kit and its use (see Chapter 12, page 91, of *Help America Read*).
4. Acquaint them with sample plans for working with children.

Preparing for the session:

1. Prepare orientation packets and gather materials.
2. Make transparencies.
3. Review chapters 1, 2, 3, and 12 of *Help America Read*.
4. Prepare a sample volunteer tool kit (see Chapter 12 of *Help America Read*).

Materials needed for the session:

- Orientation Packet (see Chapter 3 of this guide)
- *Help America Read: A Handbook for Volunteers*
- Transparencies: Meeting the Child, Reading Aloud to Children, Ten Ways Literacy Volunteers Can Help Children, and Suggestions for Effective Sessions
- A book to read aloud to the group and a child (use the same book for both)
- Notebook for each participant
- Selection of books to read aloud

Schedule

1. *Orientation* (60 minutes)

- Distribute Orientation Packet and *Help America Read*.
- Introduce volunteers and staff members.
- Provide a brief overview.
- Give information about the nuts and bolts of the program.
- Discuss location and schedule for training.
- Provide a tour of the building.

2. *Using the handbook,* Help America Read

- Distribute the handbook.
- Explain that the handbook will be a resource to read independently and refer to during training sessions.

3. *Meeting the child*

- Make three or four key points on how to meet and get to know the child or children.

USE TRANSPARENCY: MEETING THE CHILD

- Talk about each of the points briefly and then refer participants to pages 12–13 of Chapter 3 in *Help America Read*.
- Ask them to look at the list of suggestions on pages 12–13, Chapter 3, "Finding Ways to Talk with Children."

4. Read a book.

- Read a short, good book from the volunteers' collection and recommend that they use a book like this one to break the ice with the child.
- Tell volunteers that there are some sample books for them to look at after the session. Refer them to Appendix A: Books Too Good to Miss in *Help America Read*.

5. Reading aloud to children

- If possible, bring in a child and read the same book, sitting beside the child and demonstrating the process (see Chapter 4 in *Help America Read*). If a child is unavailable, we recommend using a videotape of yourself reading to a child.
- Ask the participants to comment on what they observed as you read to the child.
- Make several key points on reading aloud.

USE TRANSPARENCY: READING ALOUD TO CHILDREN

- Recommended: Send participants in pairs to read to a child (use process described in Chapter 4). Discuss the experience afterwards. If this is not possible in the training session, arrange for these experiences to take place during the first few weeks of volunteering.

6. Introduction to the ten ways literacy volunteers can help children.

- Refer participants to the organizing chart on the inside cover of the handbook.

USE TRANSPARENCY: TEN WAYS LITERACY VOLUNTEERS CAN HELP CHILDREN

- Make the following points:

   1) This chart provides a variety of ways to work with children in literacy learning.
   2) The training program will help them understand and apply each way effectively.
   3) The demonstration of reading aloud was a brief introduction to one of the ways.
   4) Chapter 2 of *Help America Read* provides an overview of each of the ten ways literacy volunteers can help children.
   5) Ask them to read and review Chapter 2 following the session.

7. Tool kit

- Show the sample tool kit and the kinds of materials they will want to use with children (see Chapter 12 in *Help America Read*).
- Talk about all of the materials in the tool kit and explain their use.
- Ideally, you will furnish a tool kit for each volunteer. If so, let them explore their own materials for a few minutes.
- Talk about where you will keep the tool kit in the setting for service.
- Suggest possible resources for adding to and replacing materials in the tool kit.
- Call their attention to the picture of the tool kit on page 92 of Chapter 12 in *Help America Read* and suggest that they read the section that describes it.
- Point out Appendix B of *Help America Read*, where we include a list of paperback books for each grade level.

8. *Sample plans*

- Help volunteers understand the need to create a very simple structure for the 30 to 45 minutes they work with a child.
- You may want to make transparencies of some of the sample plans in *Help America Read*.
- Direct volunteers' attention to the pages of sample plans in Chapter 12 of *Help America Read*.
- Talk through what would happen in a session for several of the plans.
- Sum up this section by making suggestions for a successful session with children.

USE TRANSPARENCY: SUGGESTIONS FOR EFFECTIVE SESSIONS

9. *Assessing your work with children*

- Point out that each chapter of the handbook ends with a list of questions that invites them to think about their work with children. Explain that they will be more effective tutors if they prepare informal written records and simple written plans for every tutoring session.
- Encourage the volunteers to have a notebook for writing observations and plans for sessions. If you have resources, it is best to give each volunteer a special notebook for this purpose.

10. *Questions* (10 minutes)

After the session

- Be available for individuals to ask questions and discuss schedules.

Evaluate the session.

EXPANDING CHILDREN'S LANGUAGE

Time: Approximately 2 to 3 hours

Goals:

- To help volunteers realize the value of conversation.
- To help volunteers appreciate children's language learning.
- To help volunteers become more sensitive to and appreciative of variations in language.
- To train volunteers to use some techniques for talking with children.

Preparing for the session:

1. Review Chapter 3 of *Help America Read.*
2. Volunteers will have started working with children. Prior to the session, ask volunteers to come to the session with information they have learned about "their" child and his language. Refer them to Chapter 3 in *Help America Read*, "Can We Talk?"; see specifically "Getting to Know the Child," "Opening a Conversation," and "Talking About Books."
3. Gather materials.
4. Make Transparencies.
5. Make a book about a child you are working with.

Materials needed for the session:

- Chart paper, markers and tape
- A selection of books from Appendix A: Books Too Good to Miss in *Help America Read*
- A world map or globe
- *Help America Read: A Handbook for Volunteers*
- Transparencies: Expanding Children's Language (2)
- Transparencies: Working with English Learners (2)
- Example: a handmade book about a child

Schedule

1. *What languages are represented in the group?*

- Ask the volunteers make a list of all the languages that their students speak.
- Ask them to write a brief list of what they know about each of the different cultures represented. (The idea is to realize what they do know and motivate them to learn more as they continue in their work.)
- Look at a globe or world map to find the places where the languages and cultures originated.

2. *Share observations.*

- Ask the volunteers to share what they have found out about the children with whom they work.

- Generate ideas: What are some interesting topics for reading and writing and conversation?

3. Review some principles for talking with children.

USE TRANSPARENCIES: EXPANDING CHILDREN'S LANGUAGE (2)

4. Recommended
Show a short videotape (about 5 minutes) of yourself working with a child in writing or book making. Invite volunteers to talk about the language you used in your interactions with the child.

5. Examine books for conversational potential.

- Organize a collection of books that lend themselves to conversation. Create a collection from the list in Appendix A: Books Too Good to Miss. You can get these books from a local library.
- If you have a population of Spanish-speaking children, include books like *My House, Mi Casa,* as it provides the information in both languages. Do the same for other languages.
- Ask participants to look at several books and talk with each other about them.
- Ask them to put sticky notes in places where they think they would have a lot to talk about with the child.
- Then, ask the group to discuss the books pointing out places where: (1) good conversation could occur; (2) children could notice details in the pictures; (3) children could join in, as in shared reading; (4) children might generate topics for writing.
- Select two or three books that might be especially good to share with the English learners in the place of service.

6. Discuss supporting English learners.

- Review suggestions for working with English learners.

USE TRANSPARENCIES: WORKING WITH ENGLISH LEARNERS (2)

- Invite volunteers to share their own experiences working with English learners or bilingual speakers in the setting for service.

  What have they observed about the children?
  What have they found helpful?
  What do they need to know?

- If any of the volunteers are English learners, they might share information and insights with the other volunteers.
- Refer them to *Help America Read,* Chapters 2 and 3 for further information.

7. Suggest making a book about a child.

- Suggest that volunteers make a book about a child by: (1) using photographs or drawings of the child; (2) inviting the child to dictate something about herself for each page; (3) stapling it together and making a nice cover that includes the child's name in the title, for example, *All About Maria.* Include something about the child's native language if applicable.
- Show the volunteers, as an example, a book that you have made about a child.

8. Questions

Follow-up sessions

- Plan a session that focuses on learning about the language or cultural groups represented by students in the community and the setting for service.
- Have small groups of volunteers observe each other at work with children. Notice children's use of language.
- Observe book making or reading aloud sessions. Notice when children are using the language of books. Discuss in a reflective session afterward.

Evaluate the session.

Plan for a Series: Training Session #3
READING ALOUD TO CHILDREN

Time: Approximately 2 to 3 hours

Goals:

1. To acquaint volunteers with some good books to read aloud to children.
2. To help volunteers realize the value of reading aloud.
3. To teach volunteers some techniques to make reading aloud successful.

Preparing for the session:

1. Review Chapters 4 and 5 of *Help America Read*.
2. Make Transparencies.
3. Gather a collection of books to read aloud; consult the lists in Chapter 4.

Materials needed for the session:

- *Help America Read: A Handbook for Volunteers*
- A collection of books
- Transparency: Reading Aloud to Children
- Transparency: Looking at Books to Read Aloud
- Transparency: Thinking About Books to Read Aloud
- Transparency: Conversation During Reading Aloud

Schedule

1. *Demonstrate reading to one child.*

- If possible, bring in a child and read the same book, sitting beside the child and demonstrating the process (see Chapter 4 of *Help America Read*).
- Ask the participants to comment on what they observed as you read to the child.
- Talk about how the process would be different if you are reading to two or three children. Demonstrate how to hold the book.

2. *Talk about the values of reading aloud.*

- Make several key points on reading aloud.

    USE TRANSPARENCY: READING ALOUD TO CHILDREN

3. *Examine books to read aloud.*

- On a table, place a variety of books that are good for reading aloud.
- Use Transparency: Looking at Books to Read Aloud to review each element listed.

    USE TRANSPARENCY: LOOKING AT BOOKS TO READ ALOUD

- Invite participants to examine the books with a partner.

- Partners can discuss the questions listed on Transparency: Thinking About Books to Read Aloud.

USE TRANSPARENCY: THINKING ABOUT BOOKS TO READ ALOUD

- Invite each group to select one book from each table to share with the rest of the group.
- Show participants the basket of books you have collected around a theme (see Chapter 5 of *Help America Read*). Choose books by a single author, poetry books, concept books, information books, folk tales, or books with a favorite character.
- Talk about the collection as an example of how the volunteers can gather books, relate the books to one another, and use the books with children.
- Explain how useful it is for children to learn how to make connections from one book to another.
- Point out that there are many suggestions for selecting and organizing books in Chapters 4 and 5 of *Help America Read*. Have participants look at some of the lists.

4. Talking before, during, and after reading a story

- Point out that reading aloud provides many opportunities for sharing conversation.
- Take a single book and, using Transparency: Conversation During Reading Aloud, point out how you might use this book as a basis for conversation. Demonstrate each of the points listed. Refer to Chapter 4 for a guide.

USE TRANSPARENCY: CONVERSATION DURING READING ALOUD

- End by writing the book on a list of books that you have read with the child. (Refer to the sample form in *Help America Read*, page 23.)

5. Keeping a record of books read together

- Show the participants how to add to the list of books read with the child.
- Ask each participant to bring to the next session a book that they have real aloud to a child, one the volunteer and child both liked and enjoyed very much.

6. Questions

Follow-up sessions

- Have volunteers bring in books that they have successfully read to children.
- Look at a collection of books around a theme, like folk tales.
- Invite volunteers to share their experiences in reading to children.
- Provide another demonstration with a child or two children.

Evaluate the session.

SHARED READING

Time: Approximately 2 to 3 hours

Goals:

1. To help volunteers understand the value of shared reading.
2. To prepare volunteers to do shared reading with one or two children.

Preparing for the session:

1. Review Chapter 6 of *Help America Read*.
2. Make Transparencies.
3. Gather examples of large print books, poems, etc.
4. Make a videotape of yourself engaged in shared reading with a child or arrange to have a child at the session to demonstrate shared reading.

Materials needed for the session:

- *Help America Read: A Handbook for Volunteers*
- Several examples of enlarged texts
- Transparencies: Shared Reading (2)
- Transparency: Progression of Support in Helping Children During Shared Reading

Schedule

1. Introduce shared reading.

Using Transparencies: Shared Reading (2), talk about the many values of reading with children.

USE TRANSPARENCIES: SHARED READING (2)

- Demonstrate shared reading with a child or show a short videotape of yourself helping a child with shared reading.
- Invite volunteers to talk about what they noticed in the child's behavior. They might: (1) notice the parts of the book that the child was able to read; (2) notice how the child's behavior changed when he was joining in on the reading; (3) look for evidence of the child's learning about print and words and how they work; (4) notice how both you and the child were enjoying the activity.
- One of the purposes of shared reading is to help children learn to match voice and print while reading left to right. Demonstrate how you would work with the child at each phase of learning. Use Transparency: Progression of Support in Helping Children During Shared Reading.

USE TRANSPARENCY: PROGRESSION OF SUPPORT IN HELPING CHILDREN DURING SHARED READING

Progression of Support in Helping Children During Shared Reading:

- **Precise pointing.** Using a finger or small pointer, point precisely *under* each word, moving left to right, while reading the words. Be sure the child can see the print at all times. Invite the child to join in. When children are just beginning to learn about print, they need this supporting finger or pointer to help them match the words they say with the clusters of letters on the page. As they begin to read for themselves, they also should point.

- **Sliding.** Slide the pointer under the words, moving from left to right so that the reading moves along a little quicker. When children can easily control precise finger pointing on several lines of text, this sliding will help to guide the eyes and will also help the reading become more fluent. You will not need to slide the pointer for very long.
- **Marking the line.** Place a pointer or finger at the left margin next to each line the child will read. Move the pointer down as each line is completed. When children can control the process with their eyes, they may still need a little support to be assured they are on the right line to keep reading in unison.
- **No pointing.** Drop pointing altogether when the child controls the process.

2. *Selecting books for shared reading*

- Find as many books as you can from the list of books for shared reading in Chapter 6 of *Help America Read*.
- Let participants look through the books to find the easy parts that children could read in unison.
- Point out that they may have to read the book several times before the child can fully participate in the sections they will read together.

3. *Examples of other materials for shared reading*

- Show some good examples of poems, rhymes, or songs that you can use for shared reading. Print these clearly as enlarged texts (no larger than 18 x 24).
- Refer to the drawing of *Mary Had a Little Lamb*, a sample poster shown in Chapter 6.
- Remind volunteers that if they print out poems or rhymes, they should use the printing style recommended at the school or the one in Chapter 8, page 47, of *Help America Read*.
- Invite them to think of some rhymes, songs, and poems that would be good for shared reading.

4. *Questions*

Follow-up sessions

- Invite volunteers bring in something that they have successfully used for shared reading and talk about their experiences.
- Conduct another demonstration of shared reading by yourself or invite one of the volunteers to demonstrate.
- Demonstrate shared reading with two or three children.

Evaluate the session.

HELPING CHILDREN READ

Time: Approximately 2 to 3 hours

Goals:

1. To help volunteers understand more about the process of learning to read.
2. To help volunteers learn how to listen effectively to children read and to learn how to support children's efforts to read.

Preparing for the session:

1. Review Chapter 7 of *Help America Read*.
2. Make Transparencies and Handout.

Materials needed for the session:

- *Help America Read: A Handbook for Volunteers*
- Transparency and Handout: "Ron's Letter"[1]
- Transparency: Coordinator Reference Sheet
- Transparency: Information Readers Use
- Transparencies: Helping Children Read (2)
- Transparency: Helping Children Use Information When They Read
- Transparency: Prompts to Help Children in Reading

Schedule

1. *Explore the reading process.*

- Give each person a copy of Ron's Letter.
- Ask participants to read the letter, helping each other if necessary.
- Read the letter together as a group, using Transparency: Ron's Letter.

USE TRANSPARENCY: RON'S LETTER

- Using the Transparency, talk about how they solved problems in reading the letter. What kinds of information did they use? Make a list on chart paper.
- Expect them to understand and identify that they:

  - slowed down to look more carefully at the word
  - thought about what would make sense
  - used background knowledge to understand or predict
  - stopped if it didn't sound right and started over
  - recognized part of a word
  - thought of a similar word
  - sounded out the first parts of the word and thought of the rest
  - sounded out all parts of an unfamiliar word

[1]Our thanks to Justine Henry for sharing this idea to help adults understand the reading process.

- Point out that readers use a variety of information when they read, including the pictures. Help them understand that children can use information from

  - their language and their own knowledge of the world
  - the meaning of the story and the pictures
  - information about how the word looks (letters or letter patterns)
  - information about how letters and sounds are related ("sounding out")

- Using Transparency: Information Readers Use, invite participants to talk about the sources of information they used to "read" the sentence.
- Cover up all sentences except the first one. Ask participants to read it and fill in the last three words. Chances are, they will find this difficult, but they will make some good predictions.
- Reveal the next sentence, which has more information, and ask participants to try again. Share predictions.
- Reveal each sentence, each time asking participants to read the last words.
- After the reading, participants will find that they have used meaning and the pattern of language to predict. They will also discover that they used the letter–sound information to figure out the words and to check on their predictions.
- Some participants will not be able to read all of the message until the final word is revealed. (There is unexpected information in the message; for example, many garlic peelers are not pink. Also, some volunteers may not have heard of a garlic peeler.)
- Talk about and list all the information the readers used in this exercise to help participants summarize all the different information sources children can use.

USE TRANSPARENCY: INFORMATION READERS USE

2. Helping children read

- Using Transparencies: Helping Children Read (2), discuss the values of helping children read.
- Present examples of the kinds of books that volunteers use to help children read.
- Review the general suggestions for helping children read.

USE TRANSPARENCIES: HELPING CHILDREN READ (2)

3. Examining books: What helps children use information in reading?

- Two short books are presented in Chapter 7—Look at Me and Watch Me!
- Have participants look at the texts of these two books.
- Ask, "What features of these books made them easy for children to read? What makes Watch Me! a little harder?"

4. Supporting children's reading

- Explain to participants that the listener can "prompt" children's reading as a way to support them. The adult language helps children use a variety of information and check on themselves as readers. A "prompt" is a brief comment or question that helps the child attend to something that will help him as a reader. It might be an action or something to think about, or some new information.
- Using Transparency: Helping Children Use Information When They Read, talk about how each question prompts action on the part of the child.

USE TRANSPARENCY: HELPING CHILDREN
USE INFORMATION WHEN THEY READ

- Using Transparency: Prompts to Help Children in Reading, discuss each sample prompt. For each prompt, ask participants, "What is this prompt encouraging the child to do?" Don't make this task too complex. The idea is to help participants realize that what they say is important in helping the child. We want them to encourage the child to try, and to praise his efforts.

USE TRANSPARENCY: PROMPTS TO HELP CHILDREN IN READING

- See the list of prompts on page 41 of Chapter 7 of *Help America Read*. Ask participants to look at the left column, which explains the purpose of each prompt.
- Invite participants to try using these prompts when they listen to children read.

5. Questions

Follow-up sessions

- Demonstrate reading with a child. Ask participants to notice how you prompt the child and what the results are.
- Have participants make some notes when they are listening to children read. Share observations in a follow-up session.

Evaluate the session.

Plan for a Series: Training Session #6
LETTER LEARNING

Time: Approximately 2 to 3 hours

Goals:

1. To help volunteers understand how children learn letters and sounds.
2. To familiarize volunteers with some of the vocabulary associated with phonics.
3. To prepare volunteers to help children learn letters and sounds.

Preparing for the session:

1. Review Chapter 8 in *Help America Read*.
2. Make Transparencies.
3. Gather Samples of ABC books and other materials.

Materials needed for the session:

- *Help America Read: A Handbook for Volunteers*
- Transparency: Learning About Phonics
- Transparency: Vocabulary Associated with Phonics
- Transparency: How Can We Help Children Learn Letters?
- Handmade ABC book
- Published alphabet books
- Letter posters
- Magnetic letters or letter tiles
- Chart and markers

Schedule

1. *Reasons for helping children learn about phonics*

- Discuss the reasons for helping children learn about phonics.

USE TRANSPARENCY: LEARNING ABOUT PHONICS

2. *Vocabulary associated with phonics*

- Explain that many "technical" terms are used when people talk about phonics.
- Using Transparency: Vocabulary Associated with Phonics, talk about what each term means and give some examples.

USE TRANSPARENCY: VOCABULARY ASSOCIATED WITH PHONICS

- Stress to the tutors that they do not need to be experts in phonics nor use the vocabulary associated with phonics with children. These terms are provided for the tutors' background knowledge only.

3. *Introduce letter learning.*

- Explain to the volunteers that not all children need this letter work. They should check with the classroom teacher to see whether it is appropriate. If letters seem to be important and no teacher is available, the volunteer can write upper- and lowercase letters on cards, ask the child to name them, and see which ones the child knows.

- Review the list of suggestions for helping children learn letters.

USE TRANSPARENCY: HOW CAN WE HELP CHILDREN LEARN LETTERS?

4. Personal alphabet books

- Show a personal alphabet book. Point out the drawing in Chapter 8 of a personal alphabet book. Help the volunteers notice that: (1) the letter in upper- and lowercase form is on the left; (2) a picture of something beginning with that letter and the word is on the right.
- Demonstrate making a page in the personal alphabet book. Have an envelope of pictures that begin with *b* (*bear, box, bus, ball*). Say it, choose it, and glue it on the page.
- Demonstrate reading pages in the alphabet book (*Bb, ball*).

5. Alphabet books

- Put several alphabet books in the middle of the table and let participants, in groups, look at the books. Have each small group share one of the books with the whole group.
- Refer to the list of alphabet books provided in Chapter 8 of *Help America Read*.

6. Letter formation

- Draw participants' attention to the letter formation chart in Chapter 8 of *Help America Read*.
- Explain that they will use the type of printing that children are expected to use in their classrooms.
- Show how to say the directions for making a letter as you form it (for *l*, *pull down*; for *y*, *short stick, long stick*; for *b*, *pull down, up, and around*.)
- Have them practice letter formation for several letters.
- Demonstrate making a "rainbow" letter (a letter the child traces over and over using different colors of crayons).
- Demonstrate using a Magnadoodle, white board, or other surface.

7. Sorting letters

- Place a tub of magnetic letters in the middle of each table. It is best to have a full set of lowercase and uppercase letters or at least a good sampling. If you do not have magnetic letters, write letters on small cards.
- Demonstrate one type of sorting, for example, letters with tails and letters with no tails.
- Ask participants to sort letters in every way that occurs to them. Each group should have one person who records all the different ways letters were sorted.
- Draw participants' attention to page 49 of Chapter 8 in *Help America Read*, the list for letter sorting. How many of those ways did they discover?

8. Letter posters

- Show a letter poster.
- Explain how to make a letter poster.

9. *Letters in names*

- Make the following points: (1) a child's name is an important resource in learning about literacy; (2) through their names, children learn letters and begin to relate them to sounds.
- Ask participants to look at the section in Chapter 8, page 50, that discusses children's names. Look at the drawing of the name puzzle.

10. *Questions*

Follow-up sessions

- Invite volunteers to bring in examples of work they have done with children on letters. Share and discuss the examples. Share evidence of learning.
- Demonstrate computer software programs that focus on letters or on letters and sounds. Help volunteers learn how to use them with children.
- Display several commercially produced phonics games. Evaluate them: What will children learn as they play them?

Evaluate the session.

PHONICS—LEARNING ABOUT WORDS AND HOW THEY WORK

Time: Approximately 2 to 3 hours

Goals:

1. To help volunteers understand how words work and learn some basic principles of phonics.
2. To prepare volunteers to support children in using phonics as a reading tool.
3. To prepare volunteers to support children in learning words.

Preparing for the session:

1. Review Chapter 8 of *Help America Read*.
2. Make Transparencies.
3. Cut out *s* word sort cards.
4. Gather ABC books or posters made by volunteers.

Materials needed for the session:

- Volunteers: alphabet books or posters they have made with children
- Word Sort handout: cards with words that begin with *s* (one envelope with word sort set for every two participants)
- Transparency: Learning About Phonics
- Transparency: Vocabulary Associated with Phonics
- Transparency: Making Words

Schedule

1. *Review of why? and what? to learn about phonics*

USE TRANSPARENCY: LEARNING ABOUT PHONICS

USE TRANSPARENCY: VOCABULARY ASSOCIATED WITH PHONICS

2. *Share letter-learning experiences.*

- If volunteers have made alphabet books or posters with students, ask them to bring and share them.
- What behaviors have they noticed as evidence of letter learning?

3. *Explore high-frequency words.*

- Refer volunteers to the list of high-frequency words on page 51 in Chapter 8 of *Help America Read*.
- Explain that these are words that are used frequently in reading and writing. It is very helpful for children to know these high-frequency words well.
- Refer them to the ideas in Chapter 8 for building knowledge of high-frequency words.

4. *Explore the structure of words by making words.*

- Using Transparency: Making Words, review examples.

- Make some words.

  1) Place twelve pieces of chart paper all around the room. Write a title on each chart (for example, "words that start alike"). Write an example (from Transparency: Making Words) at the top of each piece of paper.
  2) Have participants (perhaps working in pairs) go around the room and place a minimum of three examples (words or word pairs) on each sheet of chart paper. The examples should fit the title.
  3) When they have finished, review each chart with the group to help them generalize the phonics principle.
  4) Explain to the volunteers that they can write words like these on cards and have children sort them according to the same principles.
  5) Advise them to ask the classroom teacher about the principles of phonics that are the subject of instruction in the classroom.

- Refer them to pages 52–53 in Chapter 8 for information on "Noticing Sounds and Patterns in Words." This resource helps children make different kinds of words with magnetic letters, notice words in their writing and reading, make lists of words that are alike, and create piles of words to sort.

5. Explore the structure of words by sorting words.

- Using the word cards from "words that start with *s*," ask volunteers to sort them as many ways as they can. Work in pairs.
- After each pair has sorted the words, discuss the principles they used to sort them.
- Stress that their sorting experience is an example of how children can learn from sorting words. They would not use this particular word sort with the children they are tutoring. The exercise will help volunteers learn how they can write words on cards and invite children to think about them.
- Collect the envelopes with words.
- Refer to Transparency: Making Words and discuss the kinds of structures that could be used for sorting words.

6. Learning phonics through reading and writing

- Return to Transparency: Learning About Phonics.
- Stress how children learn phonics through reading books and writing their own stories.
- If you have examples of young children's writing or examples of behavior in reading, share them with the group.
- Ask them to observe children closely during the next week to get examples of how children use what they know about letters and words while reading and writing.

7. Questions

Follow-up sessions

- Introduce volunteers to computer software designed to help children learn about phonics and words. Play the games and explain how to use this tool with children.
- Invite participants to bring in samples of children's writing and examine them for evidence of what they know about words and how they work.

Evaluate the session.

say	scare	scoop
scale	skate	sky
skirt	small	smoke
smile	smart	swim
swing	sweet	street
straw	squirrel	sing
snap	snow	snack
stop	spell	space

spoon	still	stay
stone	stamp	spring
sprinkle	spray	squirt
squeeze	swell	so
see	seal	sat
soap	sock	sip
sail	sand	send
sell	song	string

WRITING FOR AND WITH CHILDREN

Time: Approximately 2 to 3 hours

Goals:

1. To demonstrate interactive writing (shared writing) and the processes of writing for children.
2. To help volunteers think about how experts help novices learn a new skill.
3. To think about how they can provide clear demonstrations of writing.
4. To think about how children can gradually become involved in the writing process by using what they know in interactive writing.

Preparing for the session:

1. Review Chapter 9 of *Help America Read*.
2. Make Transparencies.

Materials needed for the session:

- *Help America Read: A Handbook for Volunteers*
- Transparency: Learning a New Skill
- Transparencies: Writing for Children (2)
- Transparencies: Writing with Children: Interactive Writing (2)
- Transparency: Observing Interactive Writing

Schedule

1. *Exploring how adults help children learn*

- Ask participants to work in groups of two or three.
- Encourage each volunteer to think of something he or she learned to do and share it with others in the group. Suggest that it might be something like driving, using a computer, cooking, or swimming. Talk about: (1) Who helped you learn the skill? (2) Did watching someone use the skill help you? (3) What parts of the skill could you do first? (4) When you could perform the whole skill, did anyone "coach" you or make suggestions? How did that help you?

USE TRANSPARENCY: LEARNING A NEW SKILL

- Refer participants to the analogy at the beginning of Chapter 9, page 57 (learning to cook).
- Ask them to read the analogy and compare it to the skills they learned and how they learned them.
- Then, address question #5 on Transparency: Learning a New Skill.
- Discuss with the whole group what these examples tell us about learning.

2. *Discussion of writing for children*

- Using Transparencies: Writing for Children (2), discuss writing for children.

USE TRANSPARENCIES: WRITING FOR CHILDREN (2)

- Using a "role play" technique, demonstrate how to write for children. Ask the group to generate a sentence about their work with children and then write it for them.
- Make a "character map" to practice:

  (1) Have them work in small groups, with one person serving as the writer.
  (2) Refer them to the character map of *Amelia Bedelia* in Chapter 9, page 59, of *Help America Read*.
  (3) The writer writes the name of a main character from a book they know (for example, *Clifford the Big Red Dog*) in the center of a circle. Draw lines from the circle outward and invite the group to offer comments about the selected character as you write their phrases.
  (4) When the groups are finished, talk about what the writer demonstrated to the group.

3. Discussion of interactive writing

Discuss the values and process of Shared or Interactive Writing.

USE TRANSPARENCIES: WRITING WITH CHILDREN: INTERACTIVE WRITING (2)

- Working with a child, demonstrate interactive writing. (If a child is not available, use a videotape of yourself with a child, or role play the situation.) A kindergarten or first-grade child will be best, because the children will not know how to write many words. Ask volunteers to observe the process, taking notes and noticing:

  (1) How was the message composed?
  (2) What did the children contribute to the writing of the message?
  (3) What did the adult write?
  (4) Was the child able to say words slowly and write letters for some sounds?
  (5) Was the child able to write some easy whole words quickly?
  (6) Did the child form some—or all—letters quickly and easily?
  (7) Did the child attend to punctuation?
  (8) What did the child learn about the writing process?

USE TRANSPARENCY: OBSERVING INTERACTIVE WRITING

- Discuss the observation, showcasing examples that show the child using his or her knowledge.
- Refer to Chapter 9, pages 62–63, in *Help America Read* and read the examples of Sharra's writing. Talk about the example, using the questions on Transparency: Observing Interactive Writing.

4. Questions

Follow-up sessions

- Ask volunteers to bring in samples of interactive writing they have done with children. Analyze the samples.

Evaluate the session.

HELPING CHILDREN WRITE

Time: Approximately 2 to 3 hours

Goals:

1. To support children as they write for themselves.
2. To help children think about and check on their own writing.

Preparing for the session:

1. Read Chapter 9 in *Help America Read.*
2. Make Transparencies.
3. Collect a few extra writing samples if you have time.

Materials needed for the session:

- *Help America Read: A Handbook for Volunteers*
- Transparency: Helping Children Write
- Transparency: Examining the Writing of a Beginning Writer
- Transparency: Writing Sample from a Beginning Writer
- Transparencies: Examining the Writing of a Developing Writer (2)
- Transparency: Writing Sample from a Developing Writer

Schedule

1. *Discussion of how to help children write*

- Using Transparency: Helping Children Write, discuss the values and processes of helping children write.
- Refer to Chapter 9 in *Help America Read.*

    USE TRANSPARENCY: HELPING CHILDREN WRITE

2. *Examining the writing of a beginner*

- Using Transparency: Helping Children Write and Transparency: Writing Sample from a Beginning Writer, invite small groups to discuss their observations.

USE TRANSPARENCY: EXAMINING THE WRITING OF A BEGINNING WRITER

USE TRANSPARENCY: WRITING SAMPLE FROM A BEGINNING WRITER

- Ask participants to turn to pages 66 and 67 in Chapter 9 of *Help America Read* that discuss how to help a child beginning to develop these early writing skills.
- Discuss how they could apply these suggestions to helping the young writer featured in Transparency: Writing Sample from a Beginning Writer.

3. Examining the writing of a developing writer

- Make the point that there are two important aspects of writing: message and form.
- Using Transparencies: Examining the Writing of a Developing Writer (2) and the writing sample on Transparency: Writing Sample from a Developing Writer, invite small groups to discuss their observations.

USE TRANSPARENCIES: EXAMINING THE WRITING OF A DEVELOPING WRITER (2)

USE TRANSPARENCY: WRITING SAMPLE FROM A DEVELOPING WRITER

- Have participants turn to pages 67–68 in Chapter 9 of *Help America Read* that discuss how to help a developing writer.
- Discuss how they could apply these suggestions to helping the developing writer featured in Transparency: Writing Sample from a Developing Writer.

4. Applying analysis to working with children

- Ask volunteers to use the questions on pages 67–68 of Chapter 9 in *Help America Read* while they help their children learn to write.

5. Questions

Follow-up sessions

- Encourage each volunteer to bring in a sample of independent writing from a child he or she is working with.
- Consider whether the child is a beginning or developing writer.
- Use the questions on the transparencies to analyze the children's writing.

Evaluate the session.

HELPING CHILDREN WITH SPELLING

Time: Approximately 2 to 3 hours

Goals:

1. To understand spelling as an important aspect of writing.
2. To learn how children learn to spell by writing.
3. To become familiar with ways to support children's spelling skills.

Preparing for the session:

1. Review Chapter 9 in *Help America Read*, especially pages 68–71, on helping children with writing and spelling.
2. Make Transparencies.
3. Gather chart paper, markers, and writing samples.

Materials needed for the session:

- *Help America Read: A Handbook for Volunteers*
- Transparency: Key Principles in Spelling
- Chart paper, markers, and tape

Schedule

1. Discussing the process of spelling

- Spelling is one important aspect of writing. It helps the reader determine what the writer is trying to say.
- It takes many years to develop a large writing vocabulary.
- What matters most is that children are improving as spellers, trying new words, and using references.
- There are three important strategies that can help young writers as they attempt new words.
- Use Transparency: Key Principles in Spelling to discuss each one and provide examples or demonstrate.

USE TRANSPARENCY: KEY PRINCIPLES IN SPELLING

- Say words slowly, listening for the sounds. (Demonstrate the process with words like *man, goat, night.* Show how the beginning speller might be able to write some of the sounds but not able to spell the whole word correctly.)
- Think of how words look. (Children need to learn to remember some visual patterns such as *they, could, meet, make.*)
- Think of other words like the one you are trying to write. (Demonstrate the use of analogy—for example, if the child knows how to write *tree* and *my*, she can use the parts she knows to write *try*. Encourage the group to think of some other analogies. Help them understand that when children know parts of words, it is easier for them to use what they know to form new words.)

2. Learning to spell useful words

- Refer to the list of high-frequency words on page 51 in Chapter 8 of *Help America Read*.
- Suggest that the volunteers observe children carefully to assess which of these words children know how to write. They can place a checkmark next to the ones the child knows and focus on helping them learn the words they do not know until the children have success with almost all the words.

3. Helping the child check for spelling errors

- Refer to the "have a try" and "look, say, cover, write, check" strategies in Chapter 9 of *Help America Read*.
- Demonstrate each strategy.
- Ask volunteers to attempt to spell the following hard words and use the "have a try" strategy:

  hemorrhage
  euthanasia
  ayatollah

- Ask volunteers to attempt to spell the words using the "look, say, cover, write, check" strategy.
- Discuss the value of helping children use these strategies for themselves.

Using Transparencies: Writing Sample from a Beginning Writer and Writing Sample from a Developing Writer, discuss the strategies children could use to learn to spell the incorrectly written words.

4. Questions

Follow-up sessions

- Encourage volunteers to examine children's writing samples to discover what they know about spelling.
- Ask volunteers to try the "have a try" and "look, say, cover, write, check" strategies with the children they are helping to write, and report the results to the group.

Evaluate the session.

Plan for a Series: Training Session #11

MAKING BOOKS WITH CHILDREN

Time: Approximately 2 to 3 hours

Goals:

1. To help volunteers learn the values of book making with children.
2. To develop skill in helping children make their own books.
3. To learn how handmade books can contribute to children's reading and writing.

Preparing for the session:

1. Read Chapter 10 in *Help America Read: A Handbook for Volunteers*.
2. Make Transparencies.
3. Make some books with children to use as examples.
4. Gather paper, scissors, glue, and pictures for book making.

Materials needed for the session:

- *Help America Read: A Handbook for Volunteers*
- Transparency: Basic Principles for Bringing Writing Materials into Children's Homes
- Transparency: Basic Principles for Bringing Reading Materials into Children's Homes
- Blank paper
- Scissors and glue for each participant
- Sample pictures cut from newspapers and magazines
- Samples of books you have made

Schedule

1. Discussing the values of making books with children

- Bring in several books that you or someone else has made with children.
- Give each small group of volunteers one book.
- Ask them to look at the books using the chart "Values of Book Making" in Chapter 10, page 73, of *Help America Read*.
- For the book they have examined, encourage each group to report one value in reading and one in writing for the child who made the book.

2. Making books

- Ask each volunteer to use the directions for a "fold book" that are provided in Chapter 10, page 77, of *Help America Read*.
- Look at Figures 10–2 and 10–3 in *Help America Read* before making the book.
- Use pictures cut from magazines or newspapers to plan and illustrate the books.
- Then, write the text for the book. Caution volunteers to be careful about handwriting. The print should match the sample for writing provided in Chapter 8. Spaces should be clear.
- Invite each volunteer to share their books with the larger group.

3. Looking at the level of difficulty

- Return to the examples shown in Figures 10–2 and 10–3. Talk about which example is easier to read and why.
- Encourage volunteers to place the books they made in order from easiest to read to hardest to read.
- Talk about the criteria they used to make their decisions.
- Make a list of some of the characteristics they looked at such as picture support, print size and spacing, lines of text, language, vocabulary, or content of the story.

4. Making a book for a specific child

- Ask each volunteer to make another book—this time, a book for a specific child she is working with.
- Keeping the child in mind, plan the book.
- Use a variety of materials—perhaps colored covers and different sizes of paper.
- Select or draw pictures.
- Write the text clearly.
- Share books with the larger group, explaining why this book will be easy for the specific child to read.

5. Discuss the usefulness and variety of book making.

- The volunteer can use all three writing techniques in book making: writing for children, interactive writing, and helping children write.
- The books that volunteers and children make together can go in the children's book boxes to be read again and again.
- Book making contributes to both reading and writing.

6. Questions

Follow-up Sessions

- Ask each volunteer to try out the book she made with the designated child.
- Report what happened at the next session.

Evaluate the session.

 A Coordinator's Guide to Help America Read: A Handbook for Volunteers by G. Pinnell and I. Fountas, © 1997. Portsmouth, NH: Heinemann. May be copied.

Plan for a Series: Training Session #12

MAKING CONNECTIONS WITH CHILDREN'S FAMILIES

Time: Approximately 2 to 3 hours

Goals:

1. To develop appreciation for children's families.
2. To help volunteers show children that they value and are interested in their families and homes.
3. To learn some techniques that will contribute literacy materials and activities to children's family lives.
4. To prepare materials that will contribute to the literacy environment in children's families.

Preparing for the session:

1. Review Chapter 6 of this guide, which describes the "writing case."
2. Review Chapters 10 and 11 of *Help America Read*.
3. Make Transparencies.
4. Make a writing case.

Materials needed for the session:

- *Help America Read: A Handbook for Volunteers*
- A writing case
- Materials for volunteers to assemble to increase home writing
- A "Mr. or Ms. Bear" backpack or some other traveling stuffed animal
- Blank journal for "Mr. or Ms. Bear"
- A few little books for "Mr. or Ms. Bear"
- Examples of writing resulting from "Mr. or Ms. Bear's" travels
- Transparency: Basic Principles for Bringing Writing Materials into Children's Homes
- Transparency: Basic Principles for Bringing Reading Materials into Children's Homes

Schedule

1. Discuss the value of increasing reading and writing in children's homes. Important points to make:

- The more children read and write at home, the more they will learn and the more they will appreciate literacy.
- When children read and write at home, they demonstrate to their families how much they know about literacy.
- When school-age children bring literacy materials home and use them, they contribute to the literacy experiences of younger siblings.

2. Introducing the writing case

- Refer to the description of a writing case in Chapter 6 of this guide.
- Show your writing case to volunteers.
- If materials are available, invite volunteers to assemble writing cases they will use in classrooms.
- An alternative option is to assemble materials for some of the simple ways of increasing home writing, as described in Chapter 11 of the handbook (for example, placing blank books or writing materials in plastic bags for children to take home).

3. Introducing the traveling bear

- Show volunteers a traveling bear (as described in Chapter 6 of this guide). You might call the bear "Mr. or Ms. Bear" or some other name. It could also be some other kind of stuffed animal.
- Show volunteers some examples of writing that has resulted from "Mr. or Ms. Bear's" going home with a child.
- Invite one volunteer to try using "Mr. or Ms. Bear" and to bring back the results.

4. Providing home books

- List and discuss ways to get more books into children's homes.
- Refer to Chapter 11 in *Help America Read*.

5. Discuss basic principles for sending home writing materials.

- Use Transparency: Basic Principles for Bringing Writing Materials into Children's Homes to guide the discussion.

USE TRANSPARENCY: BASIC PRINCIPLES FOR BRINGING WRITING MATERIALS INTO CHILDREN'S HOMES

6. Discuss basic principles for sending home reading materials.

- Use Transparency: Basic Principles for Bringing Reading Materials into Children's Homes to guide the discussion.

USE TRANSPARENCY: BASIC PRINCIPLES FOR BRINGING READING MATERIALS INTO CHILDREN'S HOMES

7. Questions

Follow-up sessions

- Invite volunteers to meet to assemble materials for home literacy use.

Evaluate the session.

Meeting the Child

- Exchange names.

- Get to know the child.

- Choose and read a short, good book.

- Set expectations.

- Make a schedule.

- Talk about how you will notify the child if you are not there.

- Give the child something to remind him or her of you and your work.

Transparency #1: Meeting the Child   *A Coordinator's Guide to Help America Read: A Handbook for Volunteers* by G. Pinnell and I. Fountas, © 1997. Portsmouth, NH: Heinemann. May be copied.

Reading Aloud to Children

Why?

- To enjoy a book with the child.

- To expand children's language and knowledge.

- To demonstrate good reading.

What?

- Choose books that have appeal.

- Choose books that you can read in one sitting.

- Consider a variety of books.

How?

- Sit beside the child.

- Be sure the child can see pictures and print.

- Share conversation while reading.

Transparency #2: Reading Aloud to Children   *A Coordinator's Guide to Help America Read: A Handbook for Volunteers* by G. Pinnell and I. Fountas, © 1997. Portsmouth, NH: Heinemann. May be copied.

Ten Ways Literacy Volunteers Can Help Children

Talking with Children

Reading to Children

Reading with Children • Shared Reading

Helping Children Read on Their Own

Writing for Children

Writing with Children • Shared Writing

Helping Children Write on Their Own

Understanding Phonics, Letters, and Words

Making Books

Connecting with Children's Homes

Suggestions for Effective Sessions

- Make a brief, written outline for your session.

- Plan for a variety of activities.

- Have materials organized and ready before you start with the child.

- Include both reading and writing.

- Make sure the child is actively engaged.

- Keep a lively pace (don't get stuck on one activity).

- Make sure the child is always successful (not struggling).

- Record notes about how the session went and list the points you want to remember for next time.

- Reorganize materials and make a brief outline for the next session.

Expanding Children's Language

Why?

- We expand our language by using it and hearing others use it.

- Through talk, children learn new words and new ways of expressing themselves.

What to talk about?

- Talk about books.

- Talk about the topic of writing.

- Talk about anything that is important and interesting to the child.

- Share your own ideas and experiences.

Expanding Children's Language

How?

- Sit next to the child.

- Make it easy to see and hear each other.

- Add to children's ideas and comments (instead of always asking questions).

- Show interest, excitement, and enthusiasm for what the child is saying.

- Use language correctly and expand on it rather than correcting the child.

Working with English Learners

Why?

- Many children speak a language other than English in their homes and communities.

- Children learn new languages easily when they have a chance to interact with speakers of the language in meaningful ways.

- Knowing how to speak more than one language is a real advantage in our society.

- Helping English learners expand their knowledge of English will help them in reading and writing.

Transparency #7: Working with English Learners: Why   *A Coordinator's Guide to Help America Read: A Handbook for Volunteers* by G. Pinnell and I. Fountas, © 1997. Portsmouth, NH: Heinemann. May be copied.

Working with English Learners

How?

- Value and know something about the children's language and culture.

- Learn a few words in the child's native language yourself.

- Encourage the children to converse even when they can say very little in English.

- Expand what they say by making additional comments so they can hear new language.

- Read to the children from a variety of picture books and talk about them.

- Invite the children to join in reading in unison when they know parts of a book.

- Use lots of pictures to help make the language more meaningful.

Transparency #8: Working with English Learners: How   *A Coordinator's Guide to Help America Read: A Handbook for Volunteers* by G. Pinnell and I. Fountas, © 1997. Portsmouth, NH: Heinemann. May be copied.

Looking at Books to Read Aloud

For each book, look at:

- Cover and title

- Author and illustrator

- Size and shape

- End pages

- Dedication

- First words of the story

- Interesting language and vocabulary

- Special characters

- Illustrations

- Humorous parts or interesting parts

- Important parts

- Last words of the story

Thinking About Books to Read Aloud

For each book, think about:

- What makes it interesting to you?

- What will appeal to children?

- How might this book relate to other books you have read or will read with a child?

- What are some new words or interesting language for children to learn?

- What might be surprising or confusing to children?

- Are there special features you will want to point out?

Conversation During Reading Aloud

- Talk about the book before reading it.

- Talk about the pictures.

- Balance conversation to keep the story going.

- Talk to support children's comprehension of the story.

- Talk after reading the story.

- Reread the story.

- Make a list of books you and the child have read together.

Shared Reading

Why?

- To demonstrate smooth, fluent reading.

- To help children learn the way print and words work.

- To experience the act of reading (with support).

What?

- Books with clear, simple print and easy-to-remember patterns or refrains.

- Poems, nursery rhymes, or songs written on chart paper.

Transparency #12: Shared Reading: Why & What   *A Coordinator's Guide to Help America Read: A Handbook for Volunteers* by G. Pinnell and I. Fountas, © 1997. Portsmouth, NH: Heinemann. May be copied.

Shared Reading

How?

- Sit beside the child.

- Be sure the child can see and touch the pictures and print.

- Read the book several times, pointing under those phrases and parts you think the child will be able to read with you in unison.

- Invite the child to join in on appropriate lines of print.

Progression of Support in Helping Children During Shared Reading

- Precise pointing

- Sliding

- Marking the line

- No pointing

Ron's Letter

Dear John:

Peace at last! Tranquility is restored so the last are left but memories. All your suggestions — great. Everything went very well because of the extensive preparations you advised. It was an excellent idea to purchase so many of the items in advance. Bulk saved money and time, so we were well supplied and even had surplus — or so I thought — a good thing too as the activity around our table became more and more frantic and all my offspring were loudly yapping at once. Luckily, I had done all the chopping, slicing, and mixing for a giant potato salad which everyone always likes. That and the ham lasted for two meals, with the grill going full time too. Thank goodness for those big cans of baked beans or we'd have had a picnic. By Sunday, though, I was breaking into the emergency supplies of marinara sauce, pasta, and frozen meatballs. The bread maker worked overtime and seems headed for a break down but no one went without. Conversation, eating, and enjoying the holiday made the occasion memorable — just as a reunion should be. Thank goodness once every five years is enough for this family!

Love ya,

[signature]

Coordinator Reference Sheet:
Ron's Letter

Dear John:

   Peace at last! Tranquility is restored as the last one left but memories still. Your suggestions—great. Everything went very well because of the extensive preparations you advised. It was an excellent idea to prepare so many of the items in advance. Bulk saved money and time, so we were well supplied and even had surplus—or so I thought—a good thing too as the activity around our table became more and more frantic and all my offspring were loudly yapping at once. Luckily, I had done all the chopping, slicing, and mixing for a giant potato salad which everyone always likes. That and the ham lasted for two meals with the grill going full time too. Thank goodness for the big can of baked beans to round out a picnic. By Sunday, though, I was breaking into the emergency supplies of marinara sauce, pasta, and frozen meatballs. The bread maker worked overtime and seems headed for a breakdown but no one went without.

   Conversation, eating and enjoying the holiday made the occasion memorable—just as a reunion should be. Thank goodness once every five years is enough for this family!

Love ya,

Ron

Information Readers Use

Read the sentences, making predictions about the last three words.

1. For my birthday, I got a new p___ ___ ___.

2. For my birthday, I got a new pink ___ ___.

3. For my birthday, I got a new pink g___ ___.

4. For my birthday, I got a new pink gar___ ___.

5. For my birthday, I got a new pink garlic ___.

6. For my birthday, I got a new pink garlic p___.

7. For my birthday, I got a new pink garlic peeler.

Transparency #17: Information Readers Use   *A Coordinator's Guide to Help America Read: A Handbook for Volunteers* by G. Pinnell and I. Fountas, © 1997. Portsmouth, NH: Heinemann. May be copied.

Helping Children Read

Why?

- To practice reading.

- To develop smooth, fluent reading.

- To figure out new words quickly.

What?

- Books children have read before.

- Easy books recommended by the teacher.

- Stories the child has written or dictated.

Helping Children Read

How?

- Sit beside the child.

- Be sure you can see the words.

- Let the child handle the book.

- Encourage pointing when appropriate; eliminate pointing when not needed.

- Support reading only when needed; let the child figure out new words.

- Don't correct too much.

- Praise both good tries and accurate reading.

Transparency #19: Helping Children Read: How   *A Coordinator's Guide to Help America Read: A Handbook for Volunteers* by G. Pinnell and I. Fountas, © 1997. Portsmouth, NH: Heinemann. May be copied.

Helping Children Use
Information When They Read

When the adult asks . . .	It gets the child to think about whether what he or she reads fits with the . . .
• Does that make sense?	• Story or the meaning (or pictures).
• Does that sound right?	• Way we talk.
• Does that look right?	• Way the word looks—letters and letter clusters and their relationship to sounds.

x

Prompts to Help Children in Reading

- I like the way you worked that out.

- Try it.

- Go back and read that again. Think of what would make sense (or sound right).

- I like the way you noticed that and fixed it yourself.

- Go back, read that again, and start the word. (Demonstrate.)

- You're nearly right.

- Do you know something about that word?

- Do you know a word like that?

- What do you know that can help?

- Look at the beginning of the word. Now, say more of the word.

Learning About Phonics

Why?

- English is an alphabetic system.

- There is a relationship between the sounds we make and the symbols on the page that represent sounds.

- The relationships between letters and sounds help us read; it is one important aspect of reading.

What do children need to learn?

- How to tell one letter from another.

- Letter names, forms, and related sounds.

- That words are made up of sounds and those sounds are related to letters and groups of letters.

- That relationships between letters and sounds can help us write words and read words.

Vocabulary Associated with Phonics

Term	Example
consonant	*b, f, s, t*
vowel	*a, e, i, o, u*
short vowel sound	*cat, pet, pig, pot, cup*
long vowel sound	*cake, eat, like, rope, use*
blends	*br, str, pl, spr*
digraphs	*ch, wh, th, sh*
prefixes	*re-, un-*
inflectional endings	*-ing, -est, -ed*
suffixes	*-ful, -ness, -ly*
plurals	*-s, -es*
upper- and lowercase letters	*Aa, Bb, Cc, Dd, Ee*
syllables	*car-ton; to-ma-to; po-ta-to*

How Can We Help Children Learn Letters?

- Make a personal alphabet book.

- Read alphabet books.

- Practice letter formation.

- Find, sort, and name letters—magnetic letters and letters on cards.

- Make letter posters.

- Learn the letters in your name.

- Put together a name puzzle.

Making Words

Make some words:

- With silent letters (silent *e*—*like*)

- That start alike (*box*, *bear*)

- That end the same (*hat*, *cat*)

- That start and end the same (*ball*, *bell*)

- With a particular vowel in them (words with *a*—*car*, *apple*)

- With beginning letter clusters (blends like *tr*—*try*, *tree*)

- With beginning letter clusters (digraphs like *ch*—*cheese*, *chop*)

- With endings (*looking*, *played*)

- With plural endings (*cats*, *wolves*)

- With one syllable (*dog*), two syllables (*rabbit*), three syllables (*kangaroo*)

- With two letters (*up*, *go*)

- With three letters (*day*, *sun*)

  A Coordinator's Guide to Help America Read: A Handbook for Volunteers by G. Pinnell and I. Fountas, © 1997. Portsmouth, NH: Heinemann. May be copied.

Learning a New Skill

- Think of something that you now can do well and then think about how you learned that skill.

- With your group, discuss the following:

    (1) Who helped you learn the skill?

    (2) Did watching someone use the skill help you?

    (3) What parts of the skill could you do first?

    (4) When you could perform the whole skill, did anyone "coach" you or make suggestions? How did that help you?

    (5) What does this example tell us about how we learn new skills?

Writing for Children

Why?

- To demonstrate the process of writing.

- To show writing is useful.

- To record children's ideas.

- To provide writing that children can read.

What?

- Notes
- Lists
- Diaries
- Story summaries
- Character maps
- Labels

- Directions
- Recipes
- Cards
- Stories
- Records
- Reports

Writing for Children

How?

- Write clearly with contrasting marker and pen.

- Be sure children can see what you are writing.

- Write in lowercase form, except where capitals are needed.

- Shape the message to make it easy to read.

- Reread each time you add a word or group of words.

- "Think aloud" about the process.

- Draw attention to letters, words, and punctuation.

- Reread the whole piece when it is finished.

Transparency #28: Writing for Children: How   *A Coordinator's Guide to Help America Read: A Handbook for Volunteers* by G. Pinnell and I. Fountas, © 1997. Portsmouth, NH: Heinemann. May be copied.

Writing with Children: Interactive Writing

Why?

- To demonstrate the process of writing.

- To show writing is useful.

- To record children's ideas.

- To provide writing that children can read.

- To give children a chance to write part of the message.

What?

- Notes
- Lists
- Diaries
- Story summaries
- Character maps
- Labels

- Cards
- Stories
- Recipes
- Records
- Directions
- Letters

Writing with Children: Interactive Writing

How?

- Write clearly with contrasting marker and pen.

- Be sure the children can see.

- Shape the message to make it easy to read.

- Reread each time you add a word or group of words.

- Get the children to say the words slowly.

- Share the pen: Have individual children write in letters and words.

- Be selective about what you ask children to contribute.

- Invite children to think and talk about the process.

- Draw attention to letters, words, and punctuation.

- Reread the whole piece when it is finished.

Observing Interactive Writing

Observe the process of interactive writing:

- How was the message composed?

- What contributions did children make to writing the message?

- What did the adult write?

- Was the child able to say words slowly and write letters for some sounds?

- Was the child able to write some easy whole words quickly?

- Did the child form some—or all—letters quickly and easily?

- Did the child attend to punctuation?

- What did the child learn about the writing process?

Transparency #31: Observing Interactive Writing   *A Coordinator's Guide to Help America Read: A Handbook for Volunteers* by G. Pinnell and I. Fountas, © 1997. Portsmouth, NH: Heinemann. May be copied.

Helping Children Write

Why?

- To enable children to write for themselves.
- To give them a process for communicating their ideas in writing.
- To help them learn more about being a writer each time they write.

What?

- Writing for a variety of purposes.

How?

- Help the children think what they want to say.
- Value children's illustrations.
- Encourage the use of references and resources.
- Encourage children to take risks.
- Help them say words slowly and write the parts they know.
- Help them check on their writing.
- Don't insist that everything be perfect all at once.
- Help them relate words to other words they know.
- Encourage the children to read and reread what is written.

Examining the Writing of a Beginning Writer

- What is the child trying to say to readers?

- Is the child using letter symbols and punctuation marks?

- Is the print written from left to right and starting again from the left?

- Does the child understand that words are made up of letters and that there is space between words?

- What sounds does the child know how to represent with letters?

- Does the child use upper- and lowercase letters appropriately?

- Does the child know how to write some words correctly?

Transparency #33: Examining the Writing of a Beginning Writer   *A Coordinator's Guide to Help America Read: A Handbook for Volunteers* by G. Pinnell and I. Fountas, © 1997. Portsmouth, NH: Heinemann. May be copied.

Writing Sample from a Beginning Writer

MOMz BIrthday

1 MY Mom iz BLLOINe Out the Cak

We Are Etting the Cak ANd the DOg Wos Syam to. 2

3 MY Mom gat a Ztt ANd FLore zhe LOVez the Ztt.

MY Mom waz there AWd dad And MADDY AMd PHLP. MY Mom WaS My. She had a GDD BIrtday. 4

Examining the Writing of a Developing Writer

First, consider the message:

- Has the child said what he or she wants readers to know?

- Has he or she presented the information in a logical way?

- Has he or she given enough information in a way that readers will understand?

- What else will readers want to know?

- Did the child tell the information in an interesting way?

- Could some of the information be left out?

Examining the Writing of a Developing Writer

Next, consider the form:

- Has the child written the words legibly?

- Has he or she left space between words?

- Has he or she written some words correctly? How many?

- Of the misspelled words the child attempted to write, are some of them spelled nearly right?

- Are there some simple, easy words the child knows how to write and can fix easily?

- Has the child used punctuation to tell the reader when to stop?

- Has the writer understood the form of writing (for example, letter, directions, story, and so forth)?

Writing Sample from a Developing Writer

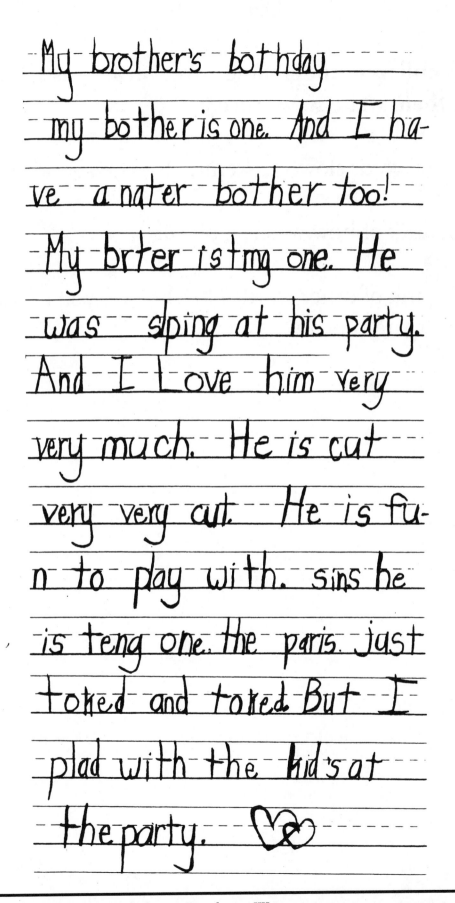

My brother's bothday
my bother is one. And I have
ve a nater bother too!
My brter is tmy one. He
was slping at his party.
And I Love him very
very much. He is cut
very very cut. He is fu-
n to play with. sins he
is teng one. the paris. just
toked and toked But I
plad with the kids at
the party. ♡♡

Key Principles in Spelling
(Clay, 1991)

Help children understand three strategies that can help them write new words:

- Say words slowly, listening for the sounds (*man*).

- Think of how words look (*the*).

- Think of other words like the one you are trying to write (*my*, *by*).

Basic Principles for Bringing Writing Materials into Children's Homes

- Select very simple materials to send home.

- Expect a product back the next day.

- Be sure the child knows the purpose for any writing materials you send home.

- Have the child practice using the materials (or materials like them) before taking them home.

- Taking writing materials home allows the child to demonstrate to family members the value of writing.

#39: Basic Principles for Bringing Writing Materials into Children's Homes   *A Coordinator's Guide to Help America Read: A Handbook for Volunteers* by G. Pinnell and I. Fountas, © 1997. Portsmouth, NH: Heinemann. May be copied.

Basic Principles for Bringing Reading Materials into Children's Homes

- As often as possible, lend the child a "read-aloud" book in a sealable clear plastic bag for the parent to read.

- Write books for the child that he or she can read and keep.

- Use inexpensive "home books" such as the KEEP BOOKS program that children can take home and keep.

- Make parents aware of sources for inexpensive, good books such as book clubs.

- Be sure the child can easily read books that are sent home for him or her to read to family members.

- Help the child select books from the school library, public library, or classroom lending collection.

- Use sealable clear plastic bags to protect books.

#40: *Basic Principles for Bringing Reading Materials into Children's Homes* *A Coordinator's Guide to Help America Read: A Handbook for Volunteers* by G. Pinnell and I. Fountas, © 1997. Portsmouth, NH: Heinemann. May be copied.

[title of your program here]

Personal Data

Name: _____ Address: _____

City: _____ State:_____ Zip code: _____

Work Phone:_____ Fax: _____ e-mail: _____

Home Phone:_____ Fax: _____ e-mail:_____

Current Occupation (if applicable):_____

References: Please provide the names, addresses, and telephone numbers of two personal references._____

_____

Time Available

How much time would you like to give as a literacy volunteer?

What specific times are you available to work with children?

Are you available to participate in training sessions? Please indicate the times you are available. The coordinator will follow up with a discussion about scheduling.

Experience

Do you have any particular experience with young children that you want us to know about?

Do you bring a particular skill or area of expertise that might be helpful to our volunteer program (for example, computer skills, knowledge of children's books or art)? Is there something in particular that you would like to do or contribute to the volunteer program?

Survey of Interests

Why did you decide to become a literacy volunteer?

What are your special interests or experiences that you would like to share with children?

What do you hope children will gain from your participation as a literacy volunteer?

What do you hope you will gain and learn from your participation as a literacy volunteer?

Sample Letter Introducing KEEP BOOKS

Dear [name of parent or other caregiver],

As you know, your child is learning about books this year and enjoying the experience. To provide more home reading, our school [or other organization] is going to provide KEEP BOOKS™, which are special books created for children to take home, write their names in, color the pictures, and read again and again.

The best place to store KEEP BOOKS is in a shoebox. So that we can prepare to send our books home, please send a shoebox to school with your child. If you have extra shoeboxes that you are not using, we would appreciate if you would send them just in case someone does not have one.

[Name of child] will begin bringing home KEEP BOOKS in about two weeks. We know that you will enjoy this new program.

Sincerely,

Sample Letter to Send Home with the First KEEP BOOKS

Dear [name of parent or other caregiver],

Today [name of child] is bringing home the first KEEP BOOKS™. We know you will enjoy reading these books with your child.

This shoebox [or other kind of box] is the best place for your child to keep the books. Please find a special and convenient place at home for the box.

Most of these books will be easy enough for your child to read to you. Reading the same book many times helps young children get the feel of reading, sound like good readers, and grow more confident. So, encourage your child to read this book to everyone in the family, especially younger brothers and sisters, as well as family friends!

If the book is hard for your child, you might want to read it together a few times so that it will become easy to read. Be sure to read the entire book rather than working on single words, because the key to learning how to read is to experience reading as an enjoyable experience. KEEP BOOKS are also good models for writing. You and [name of child] might want to write and illustrate your own books to keep in the shoebox. Pictures from magazines, catalogues, or the Sunday paper are good illustrations for these little books.

At the end of the year, we will ask you to provide some information about how your child has enjoyed these books.

Your child will begin bringing home a KEEP BOOK each week this year. We will provide ___ of these books this year.

Sincerely,

Sample Letter to Send Home with the First KEEP BOOKS   *A Coordinator's Guide to Help America Read:*
A Handbook for Volunteers by G. Pinnell and I. Fountas, © 1997. Portsmouth, NH: Heinemann. May be copied.

Sample Letter to Send Home with the Writing Briefcase

Dear [name of parent or other caregiver],

Today your child is bringing home our writing case. We want young children to "try out" writing at home. They do not have to write something that is perfect. They learn as they write. The more they write, the better they become at writing and spelling.

This case has many different kinds of supplies for writing because, after all, people use writing for many different purposes and need different writing supplies.

Help your child [for an individual letter, substitute the name of the child] select paper and other writing supplies. Your child might like to make a book or write something about himself or his interests. Help your child think of something to write about and then help him write it.

Encourage your child to do most of the writing. Saying the words slowly and thinking about the sounds will help. There is no need to correct the writing. Praise your child's efforts. Enjoy the experience.

Tomorrow, remind your child to bring the writing case back to school with a piece of writing to share.

This writing case will come home again soon.

Sincerely,

Sample Letter to Send Home with the Writing Briefcase   *A Coordinator's Guide to Help America Read: A Handbook for Volunteers* by G. Pinnell and I. Fountas, © 1997. Portsmouth, NH: Heinemann. May be copied.

Survey: Information for the Literacy Volunteer Program

This survey is designed to acquire the information we need to plan our literacy volunteer program. We will use this information as a guide as we provide training for volunteers, allocate time, and organize the program. This information will be valuable to us and we will do our best to accommodate your preferences within the limits of our time and volunteer personnel. You may check more than one response and write comments at the end of this survey.

Name:_____

Location:_____

Role: _____

1. How many children would you like the volunteer(s) to work with?
___ individual children   ___ small groups of three or four
___ pairs of children   ___ other (please describe):

2. Who would you like the volunteer(s) to work with?
___ the same children each time they come
___ any children who need help on a given day
___ other (please describe):

3. Where will the volunteer(s) work?
___ in classrooms
___ in another space to be provided (please describe):

4. When would it be best for the volunteer(s) to provide services?
___ in the mornings (indicate   ___ after-school, weekend, or evening
    best times):   service
___ during afternoon periods (indicate ___ whenever volunteers are
    best times):   available

5. What do you think volunteers can do to be most helpful to the children in your setting?
The following is a brief description of ten ways to work with children as a literacy volunteer. We also indicate the value of each way for children. Please check those you think are especially important for the children your volunteers will help. Later, you will want to advise individual volunteers about specific children's needs.

Ten Ways Literacy Volunteers Can Help Children	Benefit to Children
__ 1. Talking with Children *The adult engages the child in talk about all kinds of topics. Sometimes talk is a prelude to reading and writing.*	Expands children's conversational abilities, vocabulary, and confidence.
__ 2. Reading Aloud to Children *The volunteer selects good books and reads to one child or a small group; frequently favorites are read over and over.*	Expands children's knowledge of stories and the language of books.
__ 3. Reading with Children— Shared Reading *The volunteer and child read a book together, following the print by pointing.*	Gives children a chance to "behave like readers" and to learn important early aspects of reading.
__ 4. Helping Children Read on Their Own *The volunteer listens to one child read one book or more; usually these are books the teacher has selected or that the child has read before.*	Gives children many opportunities to practice reading.
__ 5. Writing for Children *The volunteer talks to the child and helps him decide what to say, then writes it for him, demonstrating the process.*	Provides adult help so that children can participate in producing messages even before they can write very much.
__ 6. Writing with Children— Shared or Interactive Writing *The volunteer and the child "share the pen," each writing part of a message or story that the child has decided to write.*	Gives children the chance to share in producing pieces of writing and learning about letters and words.
__ 7. Helping Children Write on Their Own *The volunteer observes the child writing a message or story and occasionally assists on hard parts.*	Provides the adult support needed for children to do their own writing.

Survey: Information for the Literacy Volunteer Program

__ 8. Understanding Phonics, Letters, Sounds, and Words *The volunteer works with children on the specific information related to recognizing letters, relating letters and sounds, and recognizing and analyzing words for reading or writing.*	Helps children focus on the specific skills they may need to learn about reading and writing words.
__ 9. Making Books *The volunteer uses all of the above techniques to help children make their own books, which they can read and take home.*	Children enjoy making their own books; this activity combines reading and writing and provides a special product that they will read again and again.
__ 10. Making Connections with Homes *The volunteer works in informal ways to send reading and writing with the children to their homes.*	Writing and reading go home and help parents understand more about their children and what they are learning.

Comments and Questions: Please provide any other important information you think we should know. Please list your questions about the ways in which our program will operate.

Survey: Information for the Literacy Volunteer Program   *A Coordinator's Guide to Help America Read: A Handbook for Volunteers* by G. Pinnell and I. Fountas, © 1997. Portsmouth, NH: Heinemann. May be copied.

Certificate of Appreciation

Awarded to

_____

for commitment to the literacy

of young children

through volunteer service

_____
Coordinator

References

Bernard, M., ed. 1990. *Volunteers in Public Schools*. Committee on the Use of Volunteers in Schools, Commission on Behavioral and Social Sciences and Education. National Research Council. Washington, DC: National Academy Press.

Clay, M. 1991. *Becoming Literate: The Construction of Inner Control*. Portsmouth, NH: Heinemann.

DeFord, D. E. April, 1996. AmeriCorps for Math and Literacy: A Federal and Private Partnership. Paper presented to the American Educational Research Association. New York, NY.

Fountas, I. C., and G. S. Pinnell. 1996. *Guided Reading: Good First Teaching for All Children*. Portsmouth, NH: Heinemann.

Lyons, C. A., and C. Griffiths. December, 1995. Exploring AmeriCorps Members' Changing Perceptions of Learning and Teaching While Participating in a National Service Program to Promote Math and Literacy for Young Children. Paper presented to the National Reading Conference. New Orleans, LA.

Neumann, A. 1994. *Volunteer Tutor's Toolbox*. Newark, DE: International Reading Association.

Pinnell, G. S., and S. Constable. December, 1995. Assessing the Impact of AmeriCorps for Math and Literacy in Two Urban Schools. Paper presented to the National Reading Conference. New Orleans, LA.

Schine, J., ed. 1997. *Service Learning: Ninety-Sixth Yearbook of the National Society of the Study of Education*. Chicago, IL: University of Chicago Press.

Wasik, B. 1997. Using Volunteers as Reading Tutors: Guidelines for Successful Practice. Unpublished paper. Baltimore, MD: Johns Hopkins University.